MY DANCE WITH THE KING OF KINGS

By FAITH GRACE CROSS

ALL RIGHTS RESERVED © COPYRIGHT 2021-2024

Library of Congress Copyright © 2018-2024

ISBN 9781734078220

Unless otherwise indicated, all Scripture quotations are taken from the King James Versions. All other versions used by permission granted or in the public domain.

"Scripture quotations marked ESV are from the Holy Bible, English Standard Version, copyright © 2001, 2007, 2011, 2016 by Crossway Bibles, a division of Good News Publishers. Used by permission. All rights reserved."

Scripture quotations marked (NLT) are taken from the *Holy Bible*, New Living Translation, copyright © 1996, 2004, 2007. Used by permission of Tyndale House Publishers Inc., Carol Stream, Illinois 60188. All rights reserved.

"Scripture quotations taken from the New American Standard Bible® (NASB), Copyright © 1960, 1962, 1963, 1968, 1971, 1972, 1973, 1975, 1977, 1995 by The Lockman Foundation Used by permission. www.Lockman.org"

*Strong's Concordance blueletterbible.org/lexicon

Caps, **bold,** underline and *italics* are added sometimes for emphasis only.

All rights reserved. Except as permitted under the U. S. Copyright Act of 1976, no part of this publication may be reproduced, distributed, or transmitted in any form or by any means, or stored in a database or retrieval system, without the prior written permission of the publisher.

However, feel free to copy for personal /group bible study, under the fair use law..

Faith Grace Cross/ email: faithgracecross@gmail.com

TABLE OF CONTENTS

Dedication	4
Acknowledgements	5
Purpose of Book/CD	6
Coming Into My Destiny	11
What's In A Name?	22
Fairy Tales VS Faith	27
Object Lessons In A Name	62
Grace By Way Of The Cross	79
A New Beginning	94
On The Road To "DWTK" CD	104
My Journal With Timeline	119
Still Dancing With My King	240

DEDICATION

I danced with **JESUS,** I danced with **GRACE**
I felt Father's **LOVE** in a warm **Embrace**
I saw Father's **Mercy** upon Jesus **FACE**
An enduring **GRACE** that comes by **FAITH**
With the presence of **JOY,** our **salvation** came
In **J**esus **O**ur **Y**eshua's name

"My Dance with the King of Kings" book and CD, are dedicated as my gift offerings to my Abba Father, the MOST HIGH GOD, who brings me **JOY, J**ehovah **O**mnipotent **Y**ahweh.

To my Savior, my salvation, my **JOY, J**esus **O**ur **Y**eshua, the KING of KINGS and LORD of LORDS.

To the Holy Spirit, the one I call my precious LOVE DOVE from ABOVE. It's amazing how you take me by the hand everyday to lead, guide and protect me. Psalm 121:5

Psalm 121:5 says, "The **LORD** is your protector; the **LORD** is the shade at your right hand." **NET**

ACKNOWLEDGEMENTS

Special thanks to all my family and friends that have encouraged me in my ministry work over the years. YOU EACH KNOW WHO YOU ARE. I'm forever grateful to you all. Shout out to my FB friends, Diana Fitzpatrick, Carla Eakes, and Edward Hughes.

Special thanks to my friend Teri Moyer for your prayers and mentorship. God sent you into my life at just the right time.

I will always appreciate YOU Diann, your unexpected calls looking after me just when I needed someone to pray with me. Thank you Robbie for being my running buddy. I love you sister.

Thanks to Pastor Glenn and First Lady Dorothy Culley. You both believed in the vision God had given me that I shared with you. Special thanks to you sister Culley for obeying God when He would lead you to call me and pray for me.

I want to give a special dedication and thanks to my sister Alice You've been in my corner always encouraging me along this journey. What I appreciate most is you laughing with me during the times there was nothing much to laugh about.

PURPOSE OF BOOK/CD

*"The **Spirit** and the **bride** say "Come". **Rev 22:17 NIV***

Jesus will someday soon return for His bride, the faithful, His elect, Israel. We just may be the generation to see Him come on the clouds. I am more than excited! I'm ecstatic, elated, and consumed with the **JOY** set ahead for all of us that are in **Christ J**esus **O**ur **Y**eshua. *Luke 21:27-28 Matt 24:30-31*

Like Noah and Lot, many of us as Christians are disgusted by the filth of this world amidst the most wicked generation of all time. The Spirit and the bride say **"Come"**. YES COME LORD JESUS!

I sense the timing is so close at hand for the wedding of the Lamb and His bride, my brothers and sisters. Are you ready to dance with the KING of KINGS? I reckon, He's more excited than any of us could ever imagine. I feel His excitement for us in my heart. I LOVE IT! The Lord is the **LOVER of my SOUL**. I LOVE HIM so much! I have written songs **riding on that excitement** in my heart.

The first moment we meet in person, face to face I know will be more than exhilarating! Heaven's atmosphere must be abuzz with all the excitement and anticipation of the marriage supper of the Lamb. The redeemed of the earth will someday soon celebrate the **wedding of the Lamb.** Much thought and preparation has gone into writing about my dance with our King Jesus (Yeshua). It's been fun working with the Lord yet there has been a lot of pain and suffering through various trials with intense spiritual warfare along the way. It took a while to understand we must share in His sufferings to share in His glory. I would like to speak frankly with you now brothers and sisters in Christ. Other than my personal testimony, you may find that much of the content of this book sounds familiar but that's a good thing. Truth is always beautiful and gratifying to lovers of truth. Whether it's in the form of simplicity or profundity, truth never gets too old to appreciate. However, it's foolish to assume everyone reading this book will be a born again believer. That being said, truth will always matter to truth seekers because we know it leads to our sanctification and the gift of eternal life. *John 4:23-24 17:3, 19*

I'm called to share my living testimony which includes some life object lessons that are for today's end time generation, appropriately called the ME generation. I can't say it enough or too many times, **"It's ALL about the MOST HIGH and, GLORIFYING HIS SON JESUS, in My Dance with the King of Kings"**.

Every step and every turn of the dance of my life was choreographed by Him. That is the case for each one of us. I hope after reading about my dance, it will prompt you to begin dancing with Him if you haven't started yet.

LET'S CELEBRATE THE BRIDEGROOM NOW AS WE CONTEMPLATE OUR WEDDING IN HEAVEN!

Christ Directed CD Project

"Dancing with the King of Kings" began as a music **CD** but it grew to include two books, a booklet and a website. It's what I call my **C**hrist **D**irected **(CD)** project. I know I didn't come up with all of this on my own. When I began writing this book the idea for a booklet came to me for the purpose of accompanying the music CD of the same name. Initially I thought the booklet would contain the song lyrics and answers to questions surrounding the songs. Maybe ten pages and at most twenty pages. But as I began writing, it developed into something entirely different and surpassed the page count of a normal booklet. It is an extraordinary book about the musical chords of heaven that declare the gospel of Jesus (Yeshua). You will find this precious book, **"Heaven's Chords"** on my new website (under construction) developed to house all the projects at mydancewiththeking.com. In Heaven's Chords you will learn about the musical chords chosen specifically by the Lord through the Holy Spirit for the making of such songs as **"Lamb of God" (The Cross Upon Calvary)** which led to the lyrics for a song titled **"Lay Him Down"**.

Music CD To Inspire

The Lord knows how much I've always enjoyed music. Perhaps that's why He inspired me to write songs. Many of the songs celebrate our dancing with the King of Kings. Lots of people make music, write songs and produce music CD's to share. They don't always tell you many, if any of the stories behind the making of their songs. The who, what, when, where, how or why questions behind some of the songs I've written I will answer in this book. There's a special message behind a particular song that's for the faithful bride church.

Then other songs for the unfaithful and backslidden called the lukewarm church, and one specifically for the lost. Some may find it interesting to know what was happening in my life leading up to the writing of a particular song. Answering these questions will lead you to where I was in my journey with the Lord, in my dance with the King of Kings.

"You Changed My Whole Life" is a special song that testifies to the tough spiritual battle I suddenly found myself engulfed in. As long as we are in these bodies living in a fallen world we will be fighting our flesh and our spiritual enemies. The Word says, 'He that thinks he is standing beware that he does not fall'. Keep your guards up! We must suit up with the **complete suit of armor EVERYDAY while praying without ceasing.** *Ephes 6:10-17*

I'm grateful for the Holy Spirit that changed me in a profound way. Many of the things I once enjoyed doing I no longer do. As a matter of fact, I hate some of the things I once enjoyed immensely. Thus, I will share some of those experiences as they pinnacled my journey through my dancing with the King of Kings. Speaking of it, deliverance is an ongoing process which can take quite some time for some. I can't explain why for some it takes longer than others. Some receive immediate deliverance as it was demonstrated in the Word. However, Jesus also explained to His disciples how some have bondages and strongholds that require more prayer and fasting.

The weapons of our warfare are not carnal, meaning we cannot fight spiritual battles in the flesh. We are assured that through God's power, might and strength we can overcome. He's a **MIGHTY God** who can and will pull down all the strongholds, He will fight our battles. He is our **REFUGE**, a mighty **STRONG TOWER** for the righteous to run. Compare *2Cor 10:3-5, Prov 18:10 Isa 9:6* Pursue holiness, pray to God daily for His GRACE to empower you to stay on the right path by crucifying your flesh daily.

COMING INTO MY DESTINY

Drawing Close To God

Throughout these pages, you'll find lessons in drawing close to God and understanding what the fear of God means in practical terms. In my dance, I learned that the proper fear of God is not based on the fear of punishment necessarily. When we aim to draw close to God, the battle ensues as we seek God's will rather than our own.

I prayed asking God to purify my heart. *'Help me Lord'*, I prayed, *'to love you and others as much as YOU LOVE me'*. The enemy doesn't want us to seek God in any way, but James 4:7-8 tells us to *"SUBMIT therefore to God. RESIST the devil and he will flee from you. DRAW near to God and He will DRAW near to you."* There's no room in the Christian lifestyle for things that cater to our fallen flesh such as anger, lust, hatred or any other evil behavior.

*[**Colossians 3:5-8 KJV**] 5 Mortify therefore your members which are upon the earth; fornication, uncleanness, inordinate affection, evil concupiscence, and covetousness, which is idolatry: 6 For which things' sake the wrath of God cometh on the children of disobedience: 7 In the which ye also walked some time, when ye lived in them. 8 But now ye also **put off all these; anger, wrath, malice, blasphemy, filthy communication out of your mouth.***

God's one on one teaching put me on the path of righteous living. We don't become perfect. I have failed too many times. But the Lord assures me of His grace, mercy and forgiveness. Genuine repentance is key but we overcome by the **BLOOD** of the Lamb, not **WORKS so that no one may boast.**

[Ephesians 2:8-9 NIV] 8 For it is by grace you have been saved, through faith--and this is not from yourselves, it is the gift of God-- 9 not by works, so that no one can boast.

What a privilege and honor it has been thus far to walk and dance closely with the Lord and learn from Him through the Holy Spirit. I anticipate it being forever! I don't take any of God's gifts or His favor lightly or for granted. To God be **ALL the GLORY forever!!!!!** For He alone deserves all the **GLORY**, **HONOR** and **PRAISE!** At times, I've thought about what I believe heaven will be like with our Lord and King, Jesus (Yeshua). I like meditating on *Colossians 3:2,* ***"Set your affection on things above, not on things on the earth."*** *KJV*

Envisioning The Kingdom

God's heart overflows with love and compassion not only for us, but for all creation. He promises all things NEW with a NEW heavens and NEW earth. *2 Peter 3:13*

When the wedding banquet begins, I imagine time will appear to stand still as we enter eternity with our new glorified bodies.

It will be a time of great jubilation and celebration as the Father and Son celebrate with us along with all creation of heaven and earth. At unexpected times I've sensed and felt His joy and peace. Can you imagine when everything culminates, all of creation will be joined together in perfect harmony to experience God's joy, happiness and peace. I've envisioned eternity in my mind's eye many times, every time I sing the lyrics of **"Come Enter the Gate"**, **"Can You Imagine" or "Dancing with the King".**

Can you envision heaven with me, of what it will be like? I'm forever grateful and thankful for the future life we will get to live with the Father Most High and Christ Jesus in the new heavens and new earth. All the **JOY** up ahead is in clear view. Can you see it? Can you feel it?

Can you see the Lord lifted high upon His throne surrounded by the seraphim who cry, **"Holy, Holy, Holy"?** *Rev 4:8* Can you see your family and friends greeting you at the pearly gate or at your heavenly mansion? The Lamb is worthy of all honor and praise to the glory of the Father, the **Most High** over all the earth.

[Psalm 83:18 HCSB] 18 May they know that You alone -- **whose name is Yahweh** -- are the **Most High** over all the earth.

Finding My First True Love

The first song I ever wrote in my life was in 1976 when I was quite young and thought I was in love. Some of you may relate to looking for love in all the wrong places. **"Don't Ever Go"** was the song title and unfortunately I lost the lyrics.

However, for now those lyrics are not important. The title **"Don't Ever Go"** speaks to the longing, insecurity and fear of abandonment I was feeling at the time and for a big part of my life. I was singing about someone whose name or face I can't even remember now. Although I don't sing the words, "don't ever go", to the Lord often, the words are faintly inscribed upon my heart as a reminder of the depth of my love for my King. Sometimes we do feel insecure about our relationship with the Lord just as King David did. Yet God assures us in His Word that He would never leave us nor forsake us.

[Psalm 27:9 ESV] 9 Hide not your face from me. Turn not your servant away in anger, O you who have been my help. ***Cast me not off; forsake me not,*** *O God of my salvation!*

*[Hebrews 13:5 ESV] 5 Keep your life free from love of money, and be content with what you have, for he has said, "****I will never leave you nor forsake you.****"*

My STORY is nothing less than OUR STORY (mine and His) together, sharing my various trials, some of my ups and downs, tears of sadness and fears of the unknown. They are mingled in with treasured moments of our love story, laced with joy, hope and laughter. I had no clue at the time that the Lord would be the answer to my heart cry for the lover of my soul when I wrote the song **"Don't Ever Go"**. It took some years, but I would find true love in the Lord **Jesus (Yeshua).** In 1977, a year later after writing my first song, I began studying the bible. I saw the Eternal Father's unconditional love and plan of salvation for mankind more clearly for the first time in my life.

I learned that God's kingdom would transform the earth into a beautiful paradise and that we would live forever in paradise on earth. It was later when I learned more about the timing of the new paradise earth. I discovered that we are seated now in heavenly places with Christ. After joining Him for the wedding in heaven we come back to rule and reign with Him on earth. This brings to light God's original purpose of paradise restored on earth to be fully accomplished through His millennial reign. Funny, I never attempted to write another song again after that first song **"Don't Ever Go"** until 2008, some 32 yrs. later. For certain, I would like to tell you my story here, for it was written by the Lord Jesus Christ, the author and finisher of our faith. I'm thankful that He doesn't reveal the contents of each chapter of our life in advance.

Although it's human nature to fear the unknown, I learned over the years to trust God who's in control. I never took my hobbies of writing, singing and songwriting seriously. I never expected that one day I would sing, write and publish music CD's. I always tried to get someone else to sing them for me. Only by God's grace could I do so and I'm forever grateful. If the Lord has given you a passion for something that only seems to be a hobby, more than likely it's connected to your God given calling.

War Room Dream

Do you have a dream in your heart that feels impossible to achieve? All things are possible with God if indeed it's His will. Glory to God! Sunday night, May 12, 2013 I prayed and worshiped the Lord until I fell asleep and I had a dream. I don't dream every night with spiritual significance but when I do dream something with a clear spiritual message I want to take note of it by writing it down. On this particular night, I dreamt that I went into a place of business where it appeared I was an employee. The person at the desk told me nonchalantly, *'Oh you are moving up to the top floor. You are being promoted'.* I looked confused and asked, *'What do you mean'?*

I was not expecting anything as wonderful as this, a job promotion! I'm not sure how the person phrased it but they said something like the boss wants you to work with Him directly. As I was riding up on the elevator to the top floor, I was contemplating what was ahead for me.

Well, I finally reached the top floor and guess who was the boss? It was my **Lord, Saviour and King Jesus Christ (Yeshua Ha Mashiach!)**

He was pleasant and kind to me, appearing happy to tell me that He wanted to train me Himself. Amazing isn't He! Yes, Jesus is training each of us through His Holy Spirit. I don't remember what He looked like nor do I remember any of the details of our conversation. Besides, that is irrelevant as far as I'm concerned. One thing I clearly remember is that He took me to the training room and said, *'Ok this is where I'm going to train you'.* Standing in front of a large flip chart board and a long pointer in hand, He said, *'Just observe me, give me all of your attention and you will learn'.* That was the end of the dream. I know God has been working on me, He knows the number one priority of my life is to experience a closer walk with Him.

As I thought about it, the classroom scenario reminded me of the opening scene in the movie **"War Room"**. Jesus reminded me of an army general pointing out warfare and combat strategy. Since the timing of my war room dream, I can see how the battle has gradually intensified. Jesus helped me to understand what it takes to be on the front line as one of His working warrior soldiers. He also put people in my life to stand in the gap for me when I couldn't pray, feeling all alone and tired in the fight. He's been the best teacher ever through the Holy Spirit helping me to understand how vital time for prayer, bible study, meditation and devotion are. It's during these times we can experience His presence communing with the Lord on a personable level. Are you utilizing some or all of these vital elements of spiritual strategy at your disposal? I will elaborate more on these strategies throughout the book. **Side note:** *Whenever I say, "you" or "your", I'm not pointing my fingers towards you, the reader, I'm including myself as well.*

Love Is Key

We can appreciate how the Holy Spirit attends to all of our needs which includes our emotional needs. I anticipate our journey continuing on into all eternity.

What more could the bride church ask for from her bridegroom. He gives her His **WHOLE HEART, OVERFLOWING** with **HIS LOVE!**

[SOS 1:2 KJV] 2 Let him kiss me with the kisses of his mouth: ***for thy love [is] better than wine.***

Love is the identifying mark of the true remnant church, the **"Pure Bride".** However, today the church as a whole is divided along racial and political lines. Did Jesus or the disciples ever bring politics into the church? Remember love is the key component we need to conquer hate, Amen.

2 Corinthians 11:2 NLT] *2 For I am jealous for you with the jealousy of God himself. I promised you as a **pure bride** to one husband--Christ.*

The Lord once told me, don't look to the left or to the right but **straight ahead** to the **LAMB that BLED**. Amen We are all challenged by this spirit of division in the world today but we can and we must rebuke and resist this spirit pitting us against one another. God has given me peace of mind to stay neutral in the affairs of national and international politics. *2Cor 4:18*

[Hebrews 12:2 NIV] *2 **fixing our eyes on Jesus, the pioneer and perfecter of faith**. For the joy set before him he endured the cross, scorning its shame, and sat down at the right hand of the throne of God.*

I'm not judging anyone nor am I telling anyone what to do regarding these issues. Remember, we must each work out our own salvation with fear and trembling. I'm merely telling you what the Lord has spoken to my spirit as I continue to dance with Him. The Lord is coming for a bride that's pure without spot or wrinkle. I am working on myself as I am being tested along these lines asking the Lord to show me more and more how to love my brothers and sisters. We're not perfect but our goal should be to get as close as possible. His love I treasure more than anything. He is the reason I share my testimony with you, my brothers and sisters.

Now, we cannot say we LOVE God and HATE our brothers and sisters, can we? It's time we all make a concerted effort of self examination by examining our relationship with the Lord and our brothers and sisters. Ask yourself as I've asked myself, "Am I relying enough on YOU Holy Spirit to help me overcome divisive issues that can hinder my progress"? Am I growing spiritually progressing toward spiritual maturity in Christ? We can know we are growing when we see His Spirit working within our soul, moving us to put His will and others before our own. *Rom 13:10 1John 4:7, 12 Matt 5:48* Perhaps, some of you reading this now are saying, 'Yes, I can relate to what you are saying'. Of course, to know God is to know He is LOVE. It is the obligation of you and I to get to know God as our personal Lord and Saviour in Christ Jesus.

Do you want more than just a surface relationship with our Creator? **Dancing with the King of Kings is a metaphor for intimacy with God.** The more intense and heartfelt our love for God is, the deeper we are willing to dig for the hidden treasures found only through intimacy with Him. Each day's a new day for insightful discoveries of our relationship with Him which can lead to profound and meaningful times of reflection. By the end of this book, you'll have direction on how you can grow, increasing in the **deeper things of God which He longs to reveal to you**.

Jeremiah 31:34 NIV "*No longer will they teach their neighbor, or say to one another, 'Know the LORD,' because* **they will all know me , from the least** *of them* **to the greatest,"** *declares the LORD.* `` *. .. will remember their sins no more.*"

[1Co 2:9-10 KJV] *9 ...Eye hath not seen, nor ear heard, neither have entered into the heart of man, the things which God hath prepared for them that love him. 10 But* **<u>God hath revealed [them] unto us by his Spirit:</u>** *for the Spirit searcheth all things, yea, the* **deep things** *of God.*

WHAT'S IN A NAME?

Depending on where you're at in your relationship with the Lord, ask yourself *"How do I begin to know Him better or possibly for some of you even at all?" "How do I grow in my relationship to know Him more intimately?"* Please reflect on these questions. One of the first things we learn about someone as we begin to know them is their name. Along with their name, over time we learn about who they are as a person. Their name carries their reputation which can be good or bad.

Graciously the Lord has openly revealed Himself in great detail throughout the bible because He wants all of mankind to KNOW HIM. However, some knowledge of HIM is only revealed to those who are willing to SEEK after Him in a profound way.

There are mysteries surrounding God that are hidden from plain sight. Yet those who long to know Him intimately are rewarded with special insight and revelations of Him. God hides Himself just enough to draw our attention to seek after Him.

[1 Chronicles 28:9 NASB] 9 "As for you, my son Solomon, know the God of your father, and serve Him with a whole heart and a willing mind; for the LORD searches all hearts, and understands every intent of the thoughts. **If you seek Him, He will let you find Him;** but if you forsake Him, He will reject you forever.

I hope you are one who longs to know God more deeply because you will appreciate the nuggets of treasure you find along the way. Some of you who are dancing with the Lord know this for yourself. If not, something may whet your appetite for more.

[Psalm 34:8 KJV] 8 O taste and see that the LORD [is] good: blessed [is] the man [that] trusteth in him.

God The Father Has A Proper Name

Jesus tells us in so many words that knowing God as our Father and what His name means to us reveals what has first place in our heart. How important is the knowing and sanctification of God's name to you? Are you willing to go the full stretch to know God which is loving HIM with your whole heart, mind, soul and strength? One significant way is by doing a diligent search of the scriptures, acquiring knowledge of Him. We will have all eternity to continue on this path of discovery. *Matt 6:9 John 17:3*

On my path of discovery I learned that God has several different names but only **ONE** proper name which is **(YHWH), Yahweh** in Hebrew and **Jehovah** in English. The shortened form is **YAH**, found in Strong's concordance in Hebrew as, **H1961 "haya"**. The root meaning of "ha**YA**" comes from the action verb, **"to be"**. Grammatically, the verb, **"to be"** in the first **person "singular"** is **"I AM"**. **YAH/YAHWEH** is the **GREAT I AM**. It's one familiar title among other titles of God.

We know that He is **singular** in being the **ONE** and **ONLY TRUE GOD.** *Isaiah 45:5* tells us, there's no God besides **HIM**. Jesus said in *Mark 12:29,* "Hear O Israel: The Lord our God, the Lord is ONE." Jesus also said, "before Abraham was, **I AM",** alluding that He was the visible representation of **YAH, the Great I AM** in the flesh. The name of **"Jesus" means "Jehovah is salvation"** and **"Yeshua" or "Yehoshua"** means **"Yahweh is salvation".** Glory to God Most High! Jesus' name is the **ONLY** name we need to call to lead us to the **Father, God Most High. All things have been subjected unto Jesus by the Father,** making HIS name the name **ABOVE ALL NAMES.** *Compare Psalm 83:18 with Phillipians 2:9-11* We can even hear the Father's name **"YAH"** pronounced in a few of the names in the Old Testament. For example: King Hezeki**YAH** and King Zedeki**YAH,** prophets Isai**YAH,** Jeremi**YAH,** and Obadi**YAH!**

Jeremiah / **whom YAHWEH has appointed**
Zedekiah / **YAHWEH is righteous**
Hezekiah / **YAHWEH is my strength**
Isaiah / **YAHWEH has saved**
Obadiah / servant of **YAHWEH**

The prophet **Jeremiah's** name means whom **Yahweh has appointed.** He pronounced the fall of Jerusalem to the Babylonians, God's judgment upon the nation of Judah.

Jeremiah told King **Zedekiah** whose name means **Yahweh is righteous**, that the city of Jerusalem would not be spared but that he would die peacefully in Babylon. [1]Zedekiah rebelled, rejecting God's word from Jeremiah, causing the loss of his sons, his eyesight, his freedom, and his throne. Through it all God was righteous and faithful to do what He promised carrying out the judgment against Jerusalem and its restoration 70 yrs later. [2]Another King of Judah was **Hezekiah,** whose name means **Yahweh(Jehovah) is my strength.** His faith was more than superficial, as his bold reforms show. Hezekiah's trust in the Lord was rewarded with answered prayer, successful endeavors, and miraculous victory over his enemies. When faced with an impossible situation, surrounded by the dreadful and determined Assyrian army, Hezekiah did exactly the right thing, he prayed. And God answered. *2 Kings 18:6-7*

Consider that God our Creator made an innumerable amount of stars in the heavens. There are billions of stars in one galaxy yet billions of galaxies in our universe. The Most High Yah is truly awesome. He calls each star by name. **Not ONE is missing! Imagine that! Astounding!** *Isaiah 40:25-26*

*[Isaiah 40:25-26 NIV] 25 "To whom will you compare me? Or **who is my equal** ?" says the Holy One. 26 Lift up your eyes and **look to the heavens:** Who created all these? He who brings out the **starry host** one by one and **calls forth each of them by name**. Because of his great power and mighty strength, not one is missing.*

There's a great example in the bible about the King of Persia, who was called and chosen by God for a special purpose. **King Cyrus** of Persia was **called by name** by God through Isaiah's prophecy. God chose **Cyrus** to conquer Babylon, for the sake of His promise to release the Jews from their captivity in Babylon. After conquering Babylon, Cyrus set the Jews free, allowing them to go back to Jerusalem, their homeland. Isaiah wrote his prophecy **150 years** before it actually happened.

*[Isaiah 45:1, 4 NLT] 1 This is what the LORD says **to Cyrus**, his anointed one, whose right hand he will empower. Before him, mighty kings will be paralyzed with fear. Their fortress gates will be opened, never to shut again. ... 4 "And why have I called you for this work? Why **did I call you by name when you did not know me**? It is for the sake of Jacob my servant, Israel my chosen one.*

Abram's name which means **"High Father"** was changed to **Abraham** which means **"Father of many nations"**. His wife Sarai's name was changed to **Sarah** meaning **"Princess"**. **What's in a name?** The evidence presented makes clear that God is purposefully motivated concerning HIS personal NAME, so much so that He puts it in His servants' names. On occasion, He assigns or changes individual names that define their God given purpose and calling. In all cases, God's name is being glorified and justifiably vindicated when necessary. God's aware of all the blasphemy being put forth against His name. He will soon vindicate His name when He pours out His wrath upon all opposers. Amen

FAIRY TALES VS FAITH

Speaking of names, it is through my name and various other aspects of my personal life that the Lord wants to teach us some **OBJECT** lessons in this book. At first, I thought Lord, people are gonna think I'm being full of myself. Yet, I couldn't overlook the fact that the Lord had called me to share my life's testimony. Clearly understanding the Lord's objective however, didn't remove the hesitancy I felt about sharing what He was telling me regarding my name and other personal details of my life. It wasn't surprising that He led me to read a minister's article one day to help me overcome this mindset.

Otherwise, it could have become a serious stumbling block to writing this book with complete honesty and integrity. The minister **(name withheld for privacy)** wrote about how reluctant he was to share certain details of his life with the public. What he said totally represented my feelings, saying that his experiences were for the purpose of teaching the body of believers. **"...Those who receive such revelation,. Are called to testify, so that others may know their calling."**

He went on to say that those of us receiving fresh revelations **must** share to **"reveal what God is doing on a much larger level."** I learned God may reveal something to us that is personal but the application is also for the body of Christ.

My goodness, after reading his article, I felt soooo much better. Better, in feeling called to testify, so that **others would understand what God may be calling them to do.** I'm compelled to share some very personal things of my life that frankly make me feel uncomfortable. But I do it for the sake of God's kingdom. The world today is at a critical point, being at a serious crossroad. We are living in a world of darkness which thrives on the darkness. Amidst the darkness, God enlightens us to see prophecies unfolding before our very eyes each and every day at an alarming rate. Moreover, we are living in a peculiar time in a place called the End Times or the last days. See *2 Timothy 3:1-5*

A Meaningful Contradiction Of Names

My name is Faye Anita Cross but my ministry name is Faith Grace Cross. You will come to understand why God gave me that ministry name. I was born Fay Anita Gray however, as a teenager, I decided to add an "e" to Fay. I learned that was God also. I discovered some meaningful characteristics attached to my name as I began writing this book. First, I learned that my name Faye means both *"FAIRY"* and *"FAITH"*. Doesn't that sound like a contradiction of sorts? It's amazing within itself that my first name would have two meanings attached that are polar opposites, yet it does serve a purpose. I've found with experience that God does everything for a reason.

When I initially discovered my name Faye means **fairy,** I cringed inside. Perhaps I was being overly sensitive but it rang a negative tone in my ears. The enemy knew how insecure I was feeling, so... he made sure I would meet a neighbor that had named her dog, of all names, Faye. That may not sound like much to you but it felt like a punch in my gut when she told me. Cmon, I know that Faye is **NOT** a common name for a dog. I stood there forcing myself to smile as she continued talking and smiling, telling me that my name Faye means **"fairy"**. Perhaps she named her dog Faye because she likes fairies? All I know is when she said that to me, my insecurities kicked into high gear. Feeling **repulsed inside,** immediately I retorted pointing out to her, 'yes, I know my name means **fairy** but it also means **"FAITH"** '.

Why would I be offended and so defensive over the words fairy and dog connected to my name? **What's in a name?** That's a question I considered a lot while writing this book and for good reasons. Names have meaning. Thankfully, today I'm not in any way offended by any of this but at the time I felt terribly offended. As a matter of fact, I'll have lots of dogs running throughout my mansion in heaven.

Spiritually Attacked In My Dream

But for now, I'm not that crazy about dogs. I'll tell you why. One night shortly before all of this happened with my neighbor, I was attacked in a dream by dog spirits.

I had never experienced anything like this before nor have I since. Yet, after that dream encounter, there was a notable increase in the spiritual attacks I began to experience. Spiritual warfare can be overwhelming for some of us. At one point I became extremely aggravated by the enemy attempting to break me. Pictures of dogs would show up on the sidebar ad space on my yahoo email account. Pics of growling dogs with long pointed teeth would pop up on the screen as I tried to catch up on my emails.

This also began to happen on my Facebook page. This would go on day after day, day in and day out. Finally, I deleted both my yahoo email account and the Facebook account. It was done to intimidate and aggravate me for sure. This was nothing compared to what I would later encounter in more spiritual battles. The Lord tells us that our fight is NOT against flesh and blood but against wicked spirits in high places. I perceived from what I had been experiencing that the enemy knew about the calling on my life and they were calling out the dogs to discourage me. Within the same week of my encounter with my neighbor telling me her dog's name was Faye someone posted a flyer on our announcement board saying, **"missing person**, last seen on **Faye Street"**. I didn't know there was a Faye St. let alone nearby where I lived. Was all of this a coincidence? Perhaps, maybe, but I saw the enemy's paw prints all over everything.

What's in a name? What is a **fairy**? For starters a **fairy** is a tiny female **imaginary** being that carries a magic wand in hand. God is not fond of the practice of any kind of magic. It doesn't matter whether it's white magic or black magic. It's all witchcraft.

What Separates The True God From False Idols

When I think of a fairy, the one thing that comes to my mind are **"fairy tales"**. Not all fairy tales are bad but in essence they are figments of the imagination. The significance is in the resulting effects or the objectives behind the stories. Hence, now's a good time to start on the road leading to an object lesson. Idols are rooted in fake notions stemming from someone's **imagination**. The idol Buddha comes to my mind. There's the laughing pot belly Buddha or some other variation of the idol made in various forms and materials. History bears out that religions promoting idol worship flourished during the 6th century. Israel fell into idol worship themselves around this time period when God had them taken into captivity.

*[Jeremiah 10:14-16 NIV] 14 Everyone is senseless and without knowledge; **every goldsmith is shamed by his idols**. The images he makes are a fraud; they have no breath in them. 15 They are worthless, the objects of mockery; when their judgment comes, they will perish. 16 He who is the Portion of Jacob is not like these, for he is the Maker of all things, including Israel, the people of his inheritance--the LORD Almighty is his name.*

*[Isaiah 65:2 NIV] 2 All day long I have held out my hands to an obstinate people, who walk in ways not good, **pursuing their own imaginations**--*

Yes, there's only **ONE true God and Creator** of all things. He declares Himself to us through His Word which is substantiated by solid evidence. He's the only God that can create and extend life with eternal life. Only the true God, the Creator can destroy both body and soul in hell. *Matthew 10:28* Once you come to know and experience for yourself that He is the essence of pure love who forgives, saves and redeems, it's then you realize what makes HIM different from all the false idols worshiped as gods. *1 John 4:3* Millions bow down to worship an image or statue called the Buddha. Buddha can't create life, nor offer eternal life or show its worshipers love and compassion. I learned Buddhists base their beliefs, traditions and spiritual practices on the original teachings attributed to a mere mortal human being called the Buddha.

[3]"The Buddha was born Siddhartha Gautama in the 5th or 4th century. He was a philosopher and religious leader who lived in Ancient Asia." [3]*Wikipedia.org/Gautama Buddha* I thought Buddha came entirely from someone's imagination but he was actually created to glorify a man named Siddhartha Gautama, who like every other human being died. No idol that man worships will ever compare to the Creator, the true God who is ETERNAL. *Isaiah 46:5-7, 9*

[Isaiah 46:5-7, 9 NKJV] *5 "To **whom will you liken Me**, and make [Me] equal And compare Me, that we should be alike? 6 They lavish gold out of the bag, And weigh silver on the scales; They hire a goldsmith, and he makes it a god; They prostrate themselves, yes, they worship. 7 They bear it on the shoulder, they carry it And set it in its place, and it stands; From its place it shall not move. Though [one] cries out to it, yet it cannot answer Nor save him out of his trouble. ... **9 Remember the former things of old, For I [am] God, and [there is] no other; [I am] God, and [there is] none like Me***

We can appreciate how bowing down and prostrating before any likeness created to represent God is idolatry. Only the true God, the God of Abraham, Isaac and Jacob should be worshiped. His only visible presence is in His Son, Jesus Christ. No idol god including Buddha can answer their worshippers prayers because they have no life in them, they can't feel, walk, talk or hear. *Rev 9:20* Over many centuries different philosophical ideologies helped to shape the various worldly religions we see today that practice idolatry. These false religious ideologies have mixed in their teachings **bits of truth** based on godly principles **originating from the Word of God, the sacred scriptures, our Holy Bible.**

Modern Day Idolatry Inside The Church

No matter how you mix it, truth mixed with falsehoods will never work. Painted pictures or idol replicas made of wood and stone or other materials convinced me that some people feel the need to have a visible representation of what they call god. Both ancient and modern day concepts of God often come out of fantasy land. The true God is an invisible Spirit. Abraham had faith in God despite the fact he couldn't see Him. Like Abraham, we walk by faith and not by sight. *2 Cor 5:7* Our faith increases as we come into true knowledge and understanding of God found in His Word. We're told in all our getting, get understanding which is wisdom based on accurate knowledge.

[Proverbs 4:7 KJV] *7 Wisdom [is] the principal thing; [therefore]* **get wisdom**: *and with* **all thy getting get understanding.**

Not one single thing concerning the true God is based on falsehoods or the figment of someone's imagination. His dealings and interactions with mankind are real, based on facts and eyewitness accounts recorded throughout history. That's as real as real can get.

*"Sanctify them by means of truth, **thy word is truth**"*
[John 17:17 KJV]

We believe in Him though we can't see Him. But if Jesus were visibly standing in front of me, my first inclination would be to bow down or do something of reverence towards Him because *John 1:1* tells me that He is God, the visible representation of God in the flesh. As popular as Jesus was in His day, there weren't many if any statues or paintings of Him in existence left behind. I suppose that's because God knew people would want to worship an image or likeness of Jesus which is a form of idolatry. Today many churches have statues and images of Jesus Christ including the shroud of Turin. We also find statues and images of the apostles and other religious figures inside churches. Members bow down before them, praying to these replicas and/or images including Mary the mother of our Lord. I know this from personal experience growing up within this denomination. I bowed down before statues of Mary and Jesus, the apostles and saints, praying to them because that's what I was taught to do. Why would the church do this knowing God is a Spirit seeking worshipers who worship with spirit and truth. *John 4:23-24*

Any Christian doing these things as a part of their worship, seeking God's presence through these measures are no different than the Buddhist who bows down before a statue or image of Buddha in their home, temple or place of worship. In all instances, this is idolatry, which is an abomination to God.

However, I don't believe God is condemning the use of images in the church for the sake of bible study and instruction used in books, magazines, slide presentations, sermons, conferences, etc. It's when we look at the images or replicas as something more than a teaching tool. When the heart gets involved it becomes a form of worship. *Exod 20:2-6* tells us what the Lord says about worshiping images or idols.

*[Exod 20:2-6 NKJV] 2 "I [am] the LORD your God, who brought you out of the land of Egypt, out of the house of bondage. 3 **"You shall have no other gods before Me . 4 "You shall not make for yourself a carved image--any likeness [of anything]** that [is] in heaven above, or that [is] in the earth beneath, or that [is] in the water under the earth; 5 **you shall not bow down to them nor serve them.** For I, the LORD your God, [am] a jealous God, .*

Safeguard Your Heart

God doesn't change who He is. *Hebrews 13:8* When God does a new thing, He will tell us. Bowing down and praying to statues and images is not a new thing God has sanctioned. He still condemns idolatry today. *1John 5:21 Rev 9:20* Israel's worship of the golden calf was a form of spiritual bondage. I would like to give one perfect example of the use of an image in today's modern world that crosses over all denominations. There's a young gifted female artist who has painted a picture of Jesus that she says she met in heaven. Many people on social media speak about this picture in terms of adulation saying this picture is indeed their Lord Jesus(Yeshua).

It becomes obvious from the things they say in their comments about the image that their hearts are attached to this mere image. In reality they are fantasizing over a picture purported to be Jesus. There's a popular video about how the painting came about.

Here's one comment out of hundreds of similar comments with a few of its replies. **Names are removed for privacy.**

<u>Comment under video about painting of Jesus</u>

*"Today I have **seen Jesus the Carpenter** the Son of the Living God."*

<u>Replies:</u>

*"Anyone else feel a sense of peace when **staring at those eyes**"*

"I'm so excited to see my savior ?"

*"**That image is the face of God** revealed in a miracle. Time will come it will topple mona liza as the most viewed painting in history."*

*"**I have never seen anything more beautiful than this. MY LORD I LOVE YOU**"*

*"I cried when the story was so magical, **congratulations on getting to know god.**"*

First I want to say I'm not judging or mocking any of these people but the Lord has led me to write about this outright idol worship of images happening inside of the church.

It's amazing that the one commenter said, **"congratulations on getting to know god."** That's the one and only thing I can say I agree with is the use of the word **"god"** in the last reply listed. Only the true God is worthy of **caps**, Amen.

The bible tells us in *1 Cor 8:5-6* that there are many... gods with a small **"g"** but only one true <u>**God**</u>.

*[1 Corinthians 8:5-6 NIV] 5 For even if there are **so-called gods**, whether in heaven or on earth (as indeed there are **many "gods"** and many "lords"), 6 yet for us **there is but one God, the Father,** from whom all things came and for whom we live; and there is but one Lord, Jesus Christ, through whom all things came and through whom we live.*

I've read many comments on social media expressing more love for the image itself than for the person. And you may say, I know the picture and I don't worship it. Yes, I understand and acknowledge that it is a beautiful painting but too many have taken it to heart that they are looking at an authentic accurate picture or representation of our Lord and Savior Jesus Christ. There's no way of proving this to be true. But out of the mouth the heart speaks. We must be careful of what takes hold of our heart. John aptly describes in Rev 4:8-11, a heavenly scene of proper worship. We know Father God's throne is in heaven and Jesus is sitting at His right hand.

[Rev 5:8 NIV] 8 And when he had taken it, the four living creatures and the twenty-four elders fell down before the Lamb. Each one had a harp and they were holding golden bowls full of incense, which are the prayers of God's people.

Also, comparing Rev 5:8 which is cited above with Rev 4:8-11 helps us appreciate the worship scene in heaven is sacred as the angels, the 4 living creatures and 24 elders expressed their praise, honor and thanksgiving, bowing down before Father God and the Lamb of God. This is an act of the heart and it's spirit led, pure true worship. We must not forget the Father desires we worship Him with Spirit and TRUTH. *John 4:23-24* So, how can we deny that sincere heart led, praise, honor and the giving of thanks for a painting supposedly representing the **REAL** Jesus, the Lamb of God is not an act of worship. Sincerity is not the issue. Serving homage to an image or idol is the real issue at hand.

How can we worship God in **SPIRIT,** and **TRUTH** while praising and giving honor and homage to an image? The truth is no one knows what God's Son Jesus, the Lamb of God really looks like. Many say they've seen Him but isn't it strange they all describe a different person. Some say He had long hair, some say short hair, with a beard, without a beard, blond hair, brown hair, tall, short or just average height etc, etc. The pure bride, the true remnant church will not worship God with the use of any likenesses of images, relics or statues because they aren't needed. It's incumbent upon us to walk by faith and not by sight. *2Cor 5:7*

Where Do We Find The True God ?

All men know the truth about God's existence which lies within their heart. They may not KNOW Him personally, but they KNOW He exists. We're assured that if we seek Him with all of our heart, we WILL FIND HIM. The evidence of His reality is right before our eyes seen in His creations. *Isaiah 9:6, 1 Timothy 1:17, Titus 1:2, Eccl 3:11 and John 17:3, Deut 4:29 Romans 1:20*

*[Romans 1:20 KJV] 20 For the **invisible things of him from the creation of the world are clearly seen**, being understood by the things that are made, [even] his eternal power and Godhead; so that **they are without excuse:***

Eternity speaks of the Eternal One, the Everlasting Father who gives ETERNAL LIFE to those putting their faith and trust in HIM. We can have complete faith and trust in the many promises found throughout the scriptures, as we come to KNOW God as ONE who can be trusted to fulfill His Word. The atheist thinks otherwise saying, God does not exist. *John 17:3* Yet, I think about how God has put ETERNITY into the heart of man. Everyone wants to live forever and never die. Only people who are sick in some way consider suicide. Those who take in accurate knowledge of God are blessed to develop a relationship with Him. Compare *Titus 1:2*

*[Eccl 3:11 NASB] 11 He has made everything appropriate in its time. He has also set **ETERNITY in their heart**, yet so that man will not find out the work which God has done from the beginning even to the end. "*

Well, for certain God's WORD has been established as truth in today's world. When we go back and look at the historical records that have been preserved down to our day, we will see the truth for ourselves. Prophecies of Jesus Christ were written centuries in advance, fulfilled in the smallest of details.

We have access to more than enough trustworthy documented eyewitness accounts in the Holy Scriptures. Even more so, many prophecies are recognizably meant for our day, unmistakably finding fulfillment in our lifetime.

The Deception of Evil Pleasures

The King of Kings extends His hand inviting you and I to dance with Him. Some refuse the invitation preferring to dance the **tango** with the devil, prancing along **enjoying the pleasures of sin.** Are we entangled with the affairs of this world to the extent of neglecting the affairs of God's kingdom? We're called to be no part of the world, putting God's kingdom first. *John 6:33 and 15:19* Because we are all born in sin, we're susceptible to dance with the devil, the god of this world, therefore we must be on guard, keeping our eyes, mind and heart set on the things above, on Jesus. **REPENT** everyday, persist in doing God's will with persistent prayer while walking in the Spirit. *1Thess 5:17* We must take a firm stand in showing whose side we're on.

Renounce Evil Pleasures (Every Negative Thought)

Amen, renounce evil pleasures and every negative thought that comes to your mind. We are to cast down these thoughts which sometimes come in as images. Yes, that's an acronym worthy of our consideration and even committing to memory. Well, it's not that God wants to withhold from His children the pleasures of life. Adam and Eve had everything they needed to enjoy the most pleasurable life but their disobedience brought sin and suffering into the world. You may be thinking, the truth still remains that **JOY** comes with serving God, for His eternal **PLEASURES** are at His right hand for our benefit despite this fallen world we live in. *Psalm 16:11*

*[Psalm 16:11 NIV] 11 You make known to me the **path of life;** you will fill me with **joy** in your presence, with eternal **pleasures at your right hand**.*

That's true but **Titus 3:3** says <u>**some pleasures are EVIL being rooted in malice, envy and hatred.**</u> Walking in the flesh, one may find pleasure in having evil thoughts towards others. The Lord wants us to understand that we cannot dance with Him and the devil. The devil was a manslayer and murderer from the beginning. He's a liar who comes to kill, steal, and destroy the truth of God's Word which we need to live in victory. In **LIGHT** of the darkness all around us, we don't have to fall under the influence of Satan's evil agenda. *2Cor 6:14 John 8:44 Rom 8:1*

[2Cor 6:14 KJV] 14 *Be ye not unequally yoked together with unbelievers: for what fellowship hath righteousness with unrighteousness? And what communion hath light with darkness?*

Evil Imaginations Thrive In A Dark World

We don't have to associate with darkness. The word malice means hatred. It's closely related to **malevolence or maleficence. Malevolence** means someone having the desire to do evil to another. **Maleficent,** the title of a blockbuster children's movie goes further in meaning. It causes harm or destruction by **supernatural** means like **witchcraft or black magic**. How can someone find pleasure in hurting anyone, yet some do. Also, many creative minds are cultivated to explore the depths of darkness flourishing in a world that consumes its contents like popcorn and cotton candy. Are we consumers? Hopefully not, because the darkness will take effect upon your life as it saturates every fiber of our society. If you play with fire you will get burnt.

[Titus 3:3 NIV] 3 *At one time we too were foolish, disobedient, deceived and* **enslaved by all kinds of passions and pleasures**. *We lived in* **malice** *and envy, being hated and hating one another.*

Our Christian walk develops as we go through a learning process. Today the enemy has the world infatuated with dark themed fairy tale like fantasies through movie cinema featured on the big screen, the internet, cell phones, video games and social media platforms.

Good triumphing over evil sounds good yet there always seems to be a hidden subtle hint of promoting evil more. The days of purely innocent fairy tales are few and far between. They're buried underneath the pretentious guise of good triumphing over evil story lines. The hidden agenda is always to contradict truth where evil appears to be harmless fun. This is promoted in TV programs, and even more so in the amusement theme parks that promote dark tales as innocent fun. The H__ Potter(HP) craze is a perfect example of the world's obsession with spiritually dark fiction employing witchcraft with white and black magic. Somehow the darkness has captivated both the young and the old. The once subtle hidden evil core is no longer concealed. The underlying evil presence of fairy tale like fantasies, comic book characters and supernatural sci-fi fiction are blatant and in your face promoting violence, hatred, deception, murder, idolatry, greed, witchcraft, magic and sexual immorality. "Once upon a time", a popular TV show once on a major network, was based on fairy tales with a profound sinister twist.

Now there are too many of this genre that come and go on some major TV networks, cable and the internet. There's a feeding frenzy for supernatural fiction that highlights the dark side today being maintained and ramped up through the clever production of high cost films for the big and small screens.

From as small as a cell phone and tablet to the gigantic plasma TV screens to IMAX screens. Professional graphic artists paint vivid scenes using 3D technology to capture the heart of their audiences. The technological advances of video/movie cinematography and graphic artistry today are astounding, appearing phenomenally eye catching to say the least. Many Christians today are reveling in the darkness of evil pleasures. It's become acceptable among believers nowadays to be entertained with dark themed books, movies, music, video games and the likes that feature sorcery, witchcraft and the occult. At one time I was looking for a Christian publisher to publish my book. I was completely flabbergasted and out done when I visited this Christian book publishing website and saw that they published books by Christian authors who wrote books with themes of the supernatural, promoting **vampires** as harmless fun. Their stories are nothing more than **dark themed fairy tales for adults.** *Rev 9:21 22:15*

*[Rev 9:21 NIV] 21 Nor did they repent of their murders, **their magic arts** , their sexual immorality or their thefts.*

*[Rev 22:15 NIV] 15 Outside are the dogs, those **who practice magic arts**, the sexually immoral, the murderers, the idolaters and everyone who loves and practices falsehood.*

Apparently they have a huge following for vampire themed books. These creative works, presenting magical artistic prose and images are designed to gain huge audiences.

They target Christians by writing these so-called Christian fantasy novels. They revel in expounding the depths of Satan. I imagine some are using the excuse of teaching the principles of light triumphing over darkness. How else could a Christian reason within him or herself that this is appropriate?

What makes a Christian write books using fantasy (falsehoods) as their landscape while planting literary seeds of witchcraft and the occult along the path of storytelling? As Christians we must be extremely careful in what we are consuming to pass our time. God does speak against this subject unapologetically in the book of Revelations. See *Rev 2:14,20-24*

*[Rev 2:14, 20, 24 KJV] 14..... teaching of Balaam, who kept teaching Balak to put a stumbling block before the sons of Israel, to eat things **sacrificed to idols** and to commit [acts of] immorality. 20 .... I have a few things against thee, because thou sufferest that woman **Jezebel** ,... a prophetess, to teach and to **seduce** my servants to commit fornication, and to eat things sacrificed unto idols. 24 But unto you I say, and unto the rest in Thyatira, as many as have not this doctrine, and **which have not known the depths of Satan** , as they speak; I will put upon you none other burden.*

As an object lesson, let's look at the world we live in which is primarily divided between two sides, **real vs fake, good vs evil, truth vs lies.** Daily we hear about the broadcast of fake news being presented as truth. Nowadays it's hard to tell what is what. Reality TV, supposedly real, is scripted, creating a fake world based on lies and deception.

Television today thrives in an atmosphere charged with poisonous fumes wreaking of evil lying spirits. Fortunately, we get to choose between the two sides of good and evil, and truth and lies. We can choose to engage in experiencing a world of imagination filled with dark spirited **"FAIRY" tales** which subtly or blatantly promote the depths of Satan, filled with **"LIES" to slowly draw us away from God.** *Rev 2:24*

Or we can choose to stand on a solid firm foundation of **"TRUTH", GOD's WORD** that promotes the love of God and His goodness, living it out through the workings of the Holy Spirit. His active **WORD** builds our **"FAITH"** in Him as we experience His goodness. We must choose one or the other, truth or lies. Which will we choose? Will we choose wholesome clean movies, books, music etc. for our past time? Or will we choose the opposite? The problem is we are born wanting it both ways. I have to admit I liked some of the reality shows and I have to pray to God to help me stay away from them because they're no good for my soul or spirit. Our natural inclination is to eat from the tree of the knowledge of **GOOD** and **EVIL**. Yet this was not God's plan for man in the beginning nor is it today. He wanted man to know and experience only the **GOOD** which was on every tree of the garden except for one tree, the tree of the knowledge of **GOOD** and **EVIL**. Eating from the one forbidden tree expelled them from the garden into a fallen world where they would live under the condemnation of sin and death. *Gen 2:9,15-17, 3:1*

Despite living in a fallen world today, **those who are living in Christ Jesus are free from the condemnation of sin and death.** *Compare Romans 8:1-2* Yet those of the world are now living under that condemnation of sin and death. Have you ever given thought to the fact that all the trees in the garden had only **good** fruit for Adam and Eve to eat, and only one with **good** and **evil** fruit? That is where the paradox lies. No pun intended. I believe it's because it was never God's intention to directly tempt Adam and Eve or their offspring with anything evil. Compare *James 1:13-17*

The world we live in is like one big garden with many trees filled with the goodness of God. However, in the midst are two distinctive trees with unique characteristics. One tree has fruit of the knowledge of good and evil and the other is a tree of only good fruit representing the tree of LIFE which is Jesus Christ. I found it interesting that after the fall, God had the tree of life guarded preventing access but there's no mention of the cherubim guarding the tree of good and evil. God's plan of salvation is clear and evident. It would come in his own timing to reverse the repercussions of sin and death. Glory to God!!! Today the tree of LIFE is now within our reach, we're all free to access the tree of LIFE, choosing Jesus as our Savior. Which will you choose, LIFE or DEATH, the tree of LIFE or the tree of good and evil? This is only my opinion.

*⁴*There is in the universe no higher aim than the glory of God in Christ; and to participate in and behold that glory means eternal blessedness. Here the eternal pre-existence of Jesus is expressly implied. John 16:24 God is eternal love. The Son is the eternal object of the Father's love, and manifests it to the world, so that it is seen in glory in His redeeming work. And it is especially manifested to those who are in Christ (John 16:27) and become obedient as He was to the Father's will (John 17:26).* ***C. Wesley E-Sword**

There's No Such Thing As Good Evil

The day is surely coming when there'll be a new world filled with righteousness, overflowing with the vibrancy of righteous living. *2 Peter 3:13* Yet, here's something to think about. Have Christian fantasy writers compromised their faith out of rebellion ensnared by the wrong tree in the guise of storytelling? They write stories that contain good but the good is canceled out by the major storyline of evil for pure entertainment purposes it seems. The fantasy writers have gathered world wide cult-like followers whose appetites are primed and ready to consume the abundance of fruits of darkness. Young and old, rich and poor, educated, uneducated, all races, and all ages are entertained by these supernatural themed narratives which are served for consumption on the world wide web and other means of media communications.

*How can **TWO** walk together unless they are in **AGREEMENT**? Amos 3:3*

We can be thankful for Jesus Christ, who breaks the chains of bondage to the things of darkness. By the Holy Spirit we can be strengthened to stay away from the tree of good and evil. Holiness and righteousness have no agreement nor anything in common with things that are evil, unclean and unrighteous. How can light and darkness dwell together? God tells us we must come out from among them, to stop touching the **UNCLEAN** thing(s) of the world. There's **NO** such thing as **GOOD** evil or a good witch the world promotes in fairy tales.

Good is good. Evil is evil. However, today the world calls good, evil and evil, good. *Isaiah 5:20* The Creator gives everyone a choice to choose good over evil, light over darkness. Truth is the rebellious ones choose evil over good and the straddlers can't make up their mind, they want it both ways. They have one foot in the world and the other foot out. As a result of doing this they choose **Baal,** embracing the god of this wicked world which will soon come crashing in on them. In *Matthew 12:27,* Jesus calls Satan **"Beelzebub"**, linking the devil to **Baal-Zebub**, a Philistine deity. *2 Kings 1:2*

[5]*"Before the Hebrews entered the Promised Land, the Lord God warned against worshiping Canaan's gods. Deut 6:14-15 But Israel turned to IDOLATRY anyway. God directly confronted the paganism through the prophet Elijah. Elijah called for a showdown on Mt. Carmel to prove once and for all who the true God was, Yahweh or Baal. All day long the 450*

prophets of Baal called on their god to send fire from heaven, surely an easy task for a god associated with the lightning bolts but "there was no response, no one answered, no one paid attention." 1 Kings 18:29 After Baal's prophets gave up, Elijah prayed a simple prayer, and God answered immediately with fire from heaven. The evidence was overwhelming and the people fell prostrate and cried, The **LORD** *(***YAHWEH***) he is God! The LORD-he is GOD"*

5*The Baalim of the Old Testament were nothing more than demons masquerading as gods, and all idolatry is ultimately devil-worship." https://www.gotquestions.org/who-Baal.html

Today there's a showdown between Baal worshippers and the true God worshippers. Baal worshippers in essence have chosen Baal the ruling godfather of this world as their god. They embrace the prostitute **Babylon the Great, the "FAIRY"** godmother of lies and deception which are deeply rooted in the **evil imagination of Baal.** Rev 18:2-5 Even the **REALITY** of the world they've chosen to be friends with has been created for them by demons masquerading as gods, who work for the devil, the god of this world. *2Cor 4:4*

[Rev 18:2-5 NIV] 2 With a mighty voice he shouted: " 'Fallen! Fallen is Babylon the Great!' She has become a dwelling for demons and a haunt for every impure spirit, a haunt for every unclean bird, a haunt for every unclean and detestable animal.

*3 For all the **nations have drunk the maddening wine** of her adulteries. The kings of the earth committed adultery with her, and the merchants of the earth grew rich from her excessive luxuries. 4 ..." **'Come out of her, my people,'** ... so that you will not receive any of her plagues; 5 for her sins are piled up to heaven, and God has remembered her crimes.*

Some Choose To Say Nothing

The spirit of Elijah is speaking through the true prophets today saying, **follow the LORD (Jehovah) Yahweh, the true God through (Jesus) Yehoshua or Baal if he is your god**. Who in your **OPINION** is trustworthy to believe and follow?

The spirit behind Baal and the prostitute Babylon the Great, is Satan the devil, Yahweh's No. 1 enemy. Babylon is inhabited by the anti-Christ spirit. She's called a harlot or prostitute because she's sold out to the devil, and his evil world for material riches as she lives in luxury. Her illicit behavior with the world is horrendous to God because she's drunk on the blood of the saints and martyrs of Jesus. In turn the world shares her sentiments of hatred for God and God's people thereby consuming Babylon's maddening wine. The nations have grown wealthy from the dealings of her corrupt spirit. They're all drunk in bed together. Spiritual fornication and adultery. We're told to get out of her. Get out of the world. Stop consuming the poisonous wine and venom of the serpent which comes by way of the arts and entertainment and false religions of this world.

[1 Kings 18:21 NIV] 21 Elijah went before the people and said, **"How long will you waver between two opinions?"** *If the LORD is God, follow him; but if Baal is God, follow him."* **But the people said nothing.**

So, again we're reminded, we have two options facing us today because we're all susceptible to straddling the fence. Our choice is framed by our opinions of the two opposing sides. Just as the people of Elijah's day said nothing, today it is the same because the silent ones prefer to straddle the fence. Those that choose to say nothing are exposed by the light of God's Word, for their silence is understood and seen clearly by their choice of lifestyle. They are the lukewarm Laodicean church, the unfaithful wife. She has forsaken her Lord for several things, mainly for power, fame and fortune and sexual immorality.

Furthermore, her preoccupation with prosperity and self first makes it obvious where her priorities are. *Luke 12:37, Luke 16:13* But there is hope for the lukewarmers. Jesus does warn and rebuke them, saying they need to repent to be victorious as overcomers. He promises them the chance to rule with him in His incoming Kingdom. *Read Rev 3:16-22*

Yes, our actions speak loud and clear as to who we really serve. James 2:20 says, "…..*faith without works is dead*". *Some* who love this world often say nothing, remaining silent when it comes to upholding God's standard of holiness. Perhaps they are silent when it comes to sharing the gospel with the lost or defending the true standards of Christian living. On the other hand, those who don't straddle the fence unashamedly, intentionally with purpose follow the Lord upholding his righteous and holy way of living. The priority of Christians should always be the same as Jesus had, obeying God's commandments and sharing the gospel. We can share the gospel when we can or at least by supporting a ministry that focuses on evangelism. The saints are submitted to the Holy Spirit allowing Him to transform their heart and mind. Their focus is on heaven and the world to come, not on this world.

*[**Luke 12:37 NKJV]** 37 "Blessed [are] those servants whom the master, when he comes, will find watching. Assuredly, I say to you that he will gird himself and have them sit down [to eat], and will come and serve them.*

Embrace Faith

Now lets talk about the opposite end of the spectrum. **Faye** also means **FAITH**. We must take up the shield of **FAITH.** Our faith is guided and protected, dependent upon the sword of the **SPIRIT, the Word of God.** Remember, we become one with anyone we become sexually intimate with. Baal and Babylon the Great are ONE together in spirit leading the world in its spiritual fornication and adultery. The Lord has promised to not disappoint those that have put their **FAITH** and trust in Him. Putting faith in God's **WORD will block all the arrows of lies and deceptions coming from the world which is guided by evil imaginations.** *Ephesians 6:16-17*

Yes I'm naturally drawn to **FAITH** because it is the complete opposite of **fairy** tales. **Hebrews 11:1** says; *"Now **FAITH** is confidence in what we hope for and **assurance** about what we do not see."* Of course, **"SOLID FAITH"** <u>**ASSURES**</u> us that what we believe is real and not based on someone's imagination as **"fairy** tales" are. This life is **REAL** and my love for God and my relationship with Him is **REAL**. We can be confident unfulfilled promises in the bible will be realized because God's word has been proven to be trusted. His promises give us hope for a wonderful future on the basis of our faith. We're not talking about blind faith but solid faith. God substantiates his WORD with action, fulfilling whatever he says. All promises from the Lord are **REAL**.

I **assure** you, we can all **DANCE** with the **KING of KINGS** self assured by **FAITH** in the **WORD himself** who is our Lord and Saviour, **Jesus (Yeshua)**. *John 1:1* The true servants of God today are of the *ELIJAH class.* **We have chosen to follow Jesus Christ (Yeshua Ha Mashiach), the true living WORD. Jesus rejected BAAL, the god of this world rooted in the lies of Satan the devil**. Yes, Jesus, the Son of the Most High God loved his God and Father with his whole heart. Compare *Matthew 4:8-10 and John 20:17*

[Matthew 4:8 KJV] 8 Again, the devil taketh him up into an exceeding high mountain, and sheweth him all the kingdoms of the world, and the glory of them;

[Matthew 4:9-10 KJV] 9 And saith unto him, All these things will I give thee, if thou wilt fall down and worship me. 10 Then saith Jesus unto him, **Get thee hence, Satan: for it is written, Thou shalt worship the Lord thy God, and him only shalt thou serve.**

[John 20:17 KJV] 17 Jesus saith unto her, Touch me not; for I am not yet ascended to **my Father***: but go to my brethren, and say unto them,* **I ascend unto** <u>**my** Father</u> *, and* <u>your Father;</u> *and [to]* <u>my God</u> *, and* <u>your God.</u>

You will see how assured I was most of the time as you read my personal journal in the following chapters. I have laid out for you my dance steps from the timeline of my life's journey with the **KING of KINGS.** My love for God kept me at the times my faith wavered. Yet, how does this relate to you reading this now? Only you can find the lessons to be learned or at best, be reminded of some things you may have lost sight of. Considering everything, do you sense the reality of a crisis posed for the world today knowing Jesus is coming back soon? There are more object lessons to come the Lord's wanting to highlight for you. Since ancient times countless numbers of false gods and idols have been worshiped in every part of the world and it continues on even more so today in ways relevant only to our day and time.

I will touch more on the specifics of how that looks later. Hopefully, unlike the world, your reality is shaped by the hopes and visions of a new heavens and a new earth free of sin and strife? *2 Peter 3:13*

Soon, very soon, the earth will be transformed into a paradise where there's no more wickedness. Jesus is our sure fast **anchor of hope.** He has the final say in the real story, **HIS** story which is being revealed in God's perfect timing of the last days. Glory! *Hebrews 12:2*

*[Psalm 37:10-11 NIV] 10 A little while, and t**he wicked will be no more**; though you look for them, they will not be found. 11 But the **meek will inherit the land** ...*

Embrace **FAITH** as it is, a gift from God. It bears repeating that the promise of eternal life will be in a world that is unlike today's world that worships the gods and idols of imagination and wood and stone, that are rooted in evil. The world promotes the lie that this world is all there is or ever will be. The spirit encourages unbridled evil pleasures of every sort, especially sexual immorality, violence, and materialism.

*[Romans 10:17 KJV] 17 So then **FAITH** [cometh] by **HEARING** , and hearing by the **WORD of GOD** .*

Embrace Truth

The world being under the power and influence of Satan are being deceived as to what is right or wrong, good or evil. After the fall, God did instruct a people called and chosen, the nation of Israel, giving them the law of Moses. The nations around them were cloaked in deception. Today we can and should choose truth over lies, righteousness over unrighteousness, light over darkness.

God's **WORD** of **TRUTH** enlightens us in knowing what is right and wrong. *John 6:51, 17:17* There's a place on a higher plane where evil does **NOT** exist. We have access to all the fruit we want or need from the tree of life which is in **Jesus Christ(Yeshua), the true living Word.** We may freely feast upon Him, assured he'll always lead us to truth. *Isaiah 45:16-19 John 6:51 Prov 11:30 Rev 22:11 Hebrews 5:14*

We can be separate from the world in a practical way while living out our God given purpose in this world. Yes, even though evil is present, causing mayhem everywhere, we can make it. The challenge may require us to avoid consuming the bad fruit being dished out in the daily propaganda coming across the airwaves. Although we want to stay abreast of things, perhaps we should cut back or avoid altogether the fear mongering news that are filled with wars, rumors of more wars, and real threats of nuclear war.

Also, push back on consuming anything containing sexual immorality, that promotes racial hatred and discord, violence and murder, etc. Evil is everywhere and unavoidable in this present world we live in.. Much of the content in music, arts and cinema and the world wide web should be avoided. Truth is, however, if we consume sexually immoral ideas, whether it's looking at images, featured in R/MA/X rated movies, pornography in any form, we are eating from the tree of the knowledge of good and evil.

There's nothing wrong with the sexual act within itself but in the form of pornography, it cancels out the good. It cancels out the true good that God made sex to be. In fact, why would you view porn, or violence, horror and supernatural spiritually dark movies? Partaking from the tree of the knowledge of good and evil most often opens the door to the enemy, which are dark portals God wants us to avoid altogether. It bears repeating, we are told to get out from amongst them speaking of the harlot, Babylon the Great, the world system of all evil, especially sexual immorality before it's too late. This world has become a home and haven for demons.

Revelation 18:2 ....

"She has become a home for demons and a haunt for every evil spirit, a haunt for every unclean and detestable bird. For all the nations have drunk the maddening wine of her adulteries."

True believers in Christ must continually reject the idol gods of Baal. Remember the baal worshippers that were challenged by Elijah were controlled by dark spirits that caused them to cut themselves in their worship to baal. These spirits were bloodthirsty and this is evident in our world today. Much of the popular programming on cable, satellite, internet or regular TV, displays lots of blood, all for the sake of entertainment. This is no different than the barbarians that entertained themselves by watching lions tear apart and eat humans including Christians for sport.

This world system of baal under Babylon goes all the way back to the garden where the spirit of God's adversary Satan challenged God's sovereignty. In all practicality, would you want to associate in any way or be friends with the enemy of your best friend? I will never understand how Christians celebrate or associate in any way with halloween. Do you consider Abba Father Most High, His Son Jesus and Holy Spirit your best friend? That's a profound question only we can answer for ourselves. It's worthy of our consideration don't you think? God's enemy comes to kill, steal and destroy our lives, especially our future life in eternity. He's a liar, the truth is not in him. Yet the Most High and Jesus will be our cornerstone of truth and strength.

*[Isaiah 28:5-6, 14-17 ESV] 5 In that day **the LORD of hosts will be a crown of glory, and a diadem of beauty, to the remnant of his people, 6 and a spirit of justice to him who sits in judgment, and strength to those who turn back the battle at the gate.** ... 14 Therefore hear the word of the LORD, you scoffers, who rule this people in Jerusalem! 15 Because you have said, "We have made a covenant with death, and with Sheol we have an agreement, when the overwhelming whip passes through it will not come to us, for we have made lies our refuge, and in falsehood we have taken shelter"; 16 therefore thus says the Lord GOD, **"Behold, I am the one who has laid as a foundation in Zion, a stone, a tested stone, a precious cornerstone, of a sure foundation: 'Whoever believes will not be in haste.'** 17 And I will make justice the line, and righteousness the plumb line; and hail will sweep away the refuge of lies, and waters will overwhelm the shelter."*

Christ followers who embrace truth, are of the Elijah class. Elijah's anointing was tangible evidence of his close relationship with God. It speaks of his loyalty, faith and trust, determination and dedication to God. These are all godly qualities to reach for.

We're all on this journey of life learning as we follow the Lord's direction in how to weigh and balance out what is right and wrong for us individually regarding these matters. The bible tells us to study the Word of God to show thyself approved. Embrace the truth!!!

OBJECT LESSONS IN A NAME

Our personal journey can be likened to our **dance with GRACE as we stay close and remain focused on Jesus. He will lead us in the right direction if we follow His steps. That is the key, we must allow Him to lead us in the dance.** Amen. It is what it is. Some of the ramifications of being born in sin will affect us in some ways that are unavoidable even though we may not be eating from the tree of the knowledge of good and evil. We live in such a fallen world but thank God it's only temporary. In spite of the darkness God has transferred us into His marvelous light which brings me to my middle name, **"Anita".** It is the Greek form of the name **"Anna"** which is a form of the Hebrew name **"Hannah".** I was pleasantly surprised to learn that, in **Hebrew,** my name **"Anita"** means *"GRACE" or "FAVOR"*

I mentioned earlier how much I do appreciate the grace of God in my life. My testimony testifies of my profound indebtedness and gratitude of God's undeserved kindness towards me. Some of my gravest sins have sometimes come back to haunt me which you will understand as you read my journal. But the good news is that salvation comes by means of God's **GRACE**, and not by our works. Glory Hallelu**YAH!** You may get tired of hearing that word from me in this book.

Ephesians 2:8-9 NLT *8 God saved you by His **grace** when you believed. And you can't take credit for this, it is a **gift from God**. 9 Salvation is not a reward for the good things we have done, **none of us can boast** about it.*

Its amazing that God's gift of **GRACE** is extended to the world of mankind. Yes, the Lord lets the sun shine on both good and bad people. He is long suffering showing favor upon all mankind, because He doesn't want to see anyone perish in the end. *Matt 5:45* Jesus longs to extend a future with eternal life in paradise to everyone. It is a world that's far more real than the world we live in today. Sadly most don't realize it because as I mentioned earlier, they think this life is all there is. God must have known from the beginning how man would wallow in sin ignoring his call and invitation to grace. *John 3:16, Rev 9:20, Rev 2:21*

[Rev 3:3 ASV] *3 Remember therefore how thou hast received and didst hear; and keep [it], and repent. If therefore thou shalt not watch, I will come as a thief, and thou shalt not know what hour I will come upon thee.*

Moreover, many who have received His grace have too often taken it for granted, using it as an excuse or license to sin. Jesus takes direct aim rebuking them as being neither hot nor cold but lukewarm. Does your lifestyle reflect that your heart belongs to the world? We must safeguard our hearts. Ask yourself, how can I safeguard my heart away from the world? Could it be that we need to spend more time in prayer and worship? Or do we need to read, study and meditate more upon the Word?

When we truly appreciate the cost that was paid for our salvation, we would be on fire for God and His kingdom and not the kingdoms of this world. *Compare Rev 3: 15-18* Grace does however, allow us to forgive ourselves as the Lord forgives the gravest of sins and crimes. Hallelu**YAH**! People who appreciate **GRACE** know they have been forgiven much which compels them to love much. If God is for me, who can be against me. *Compare Romans 8:37-39* Do you appreciate knowing you have God's **FAVOR** on you? Let's always give thanks to Abba Father, for his loving kindness. *Isaiah 61:1-3*

*[Isaiah 61:2-3 NIV] 2 to proclaim the year of the LORD's **favor** and the day of vengeance of our God, to comfort all who mourn, 3 and provide for those who grieve in Zion--to bestow on them a crown of beauty instead of ashes, the oil of joy instead of mourning, and a garment of praise instead of a spirit of despair. They will be called oaks of righteousness, a planting of the LORD for the display of his splendor.*

Christ died, was buried and raised to life again so that we may have eternal life. His blood covers our sins. That's God's grace. If you haven't received Christ as your personal Savior and friend, I invite you to now. Receive Him inside your heart accepting His blood sacrifice for your sins. Declare that you will live your life fully for Him. Make a public declaration by telling someone of your new found faith. Read the Word daily, talk to Him daily, praying He makes His will known for your life. Get involved with a group of like minded people who study the bible and live for God. Amen

Glory to God! Now share the gospel message, the good news with others as the opportunity affords you in the work of saving lost souls. We can influence the lost by being a testimony of God's kingdom by simply letting our light shine. Studying the bible will help you to understand how the kingdom will affect your life today, tomorrow and for all eternity. His light and **favor is the gift of grace for you** to receive.

Grace is a naturally beautiful and popular name these days. There's irony in the fact that as He gave me the middle name **Anita**, He could have told my mother to name me **Grace.** He could have told her to name me **Faith** instead of **Fay.** But, then I would've never experienced the awkward situation, learning my neighbor's dog was named **Fay.** (smiling) I'd like to put all kidding aside but how can I when God shows me over and over again His sense of humor in my life...and I share the laugh with Him laughing at myself. God's ways are higher than our ways. Beyond that incident, His overall plan served a higher purpose. It occurred to me, He wanted me to look into the meanings behind my name to serve as an object lesson. And listen, it didn't stop there.

Cleansed By The Blood Shed On The Cross

I was born with the last name **Gray**. I found out something interesting regarding the meaning of my last name **Gray** which as a color is spelled two ways, **gray** or **grey**. My understanding is that the USA spells it as gray and the UK as grey. I googled it, to find it is said to be derived *"From a nickname for a person who had grey hair or **grey (gray) clothes"**.* God continues to amaze me.

When I first saw that grey(gray) clothes I couldn't believe it. Can you see where I'm going with this? It's where the Holy Spirit is leading me. Our sinful nature is like being clothed in gray clothing. The bible calls it **FILTHY RAGS.** The mixture of black and white makes the color gray. The world today is affixed on the many different **SHADES OF GRAY.** Any shade of gray has some mixture of the color black in it no matter how miniscule or small it is. A little leaven ferments the whole lump. A speck of dirt defiles a glass of pure clean water no matter how small the speck is. In the bible, the color black often symbolizes something evil, or spiritual darkness. We cannot mix the darkness of this world with the pure light of God's righteousness and holiness. *2Cor 6:14 1John 1:5 Rom 13: 12*

*[Isaiah 64:6 NIV] 6 All of us have become like one who is unclean, and all our righteous acts are **like filthy rags**; we all shrivel up like a leaf, and like the wind our sins sweep us away.*

*[Romans 13:12 NIV] 12 The night is nearly over; the day is almost here. So **let us put aside the deeds of darkness** and put on the armor of light.*

Before Jesus came, man was without any real hope of ever being truly righteous. Even when man put his best foot forward his righteousness was still like filthy rags. Because we're all born into sin our sins separate us from God. *Isa 61:10 Rev 3:5* But God...our God has changed the **COLOR** of our **GRAY** clothes (**garments**) to **WHITE**. We now have a **WHITE robe of righteousness,** because of the **BLOOD** of the Lamb. In the transfiguration, Jesus showed to a few close disciples his **GLORY,** being clothed in glistening white raiment displaying the **BEAUTY** of his **HOLINESS.** *Rev 3:5, 4:4;*

*[Luke 9:29 NKJV] 29 He prayed, the appearance of His face was altered, and His **robe** [became] **white** [and] **glistening**.*

*[Rev 19:8, 14 NKJV] 8 And to her it was granted to be arrayed in **fine linen, clean and bright,** for the fine linen is the righteous acts of the saints. ... 14 And the armies in heaven, clothed in fine **linen, white and clean**, followed Him on white horses*

Take note in the Lord's object lesson of my last name. He changed me from the name **GRAY,** changing my **(gray clothes)** garments (**filthy rags**) by way of the **BLOOD** shed on the **CROSS.** Therefore, the Lord gave me the perfect, highly appropriate new last name of **"CROSS"** through **my stepfather.** Yes, God changed my last name but what is the point? People get their names changed everyday. But, sometimes God will need to change things in our life which call for a name change like **Abram, Sarai and Jacob** .

Why? Because there's meaning behind names sometimes to fulfill a special God given purpose. I went from **Fay Anita Gray,** a person susceptible to dancing with the devil by default as we all are, being born in sin separated from God in a world saturated in false idol worship. But in spite of being a sinner, God calls us by another name, a better name. He wants us to look inside to see who we are in Him as He leads us in our dance of grace.

Therein lies the true meaning of life, to live within the parameters God sets forth for us. He adds meaning, depth, and purpose when we seek **HIM** with all of our heart. He examines the heart, then exposes what is truly on the inside to us. He reveals the issues in our life that need change and correction. Does that make sense to you? Just as he showed me the meanings and changes behind my name, FAY**(FAIRY/FAITH)** ANITA**(GRACE)** GRAY**(CROSS)** it was a reflection of who I was and was to become in **HIM** because of **HIM(GRACE). He had to transform me.**

God wants to transform us individually giving us the GIFTS of FAITH and GRACE by way of the BLOOD shed on the CROSS of Calvary.

*[Ephesians 2:8, 16 NIV] 8 For it is by **GRACE** you have been saved, through **FAITH** and this is not from yourselves, it is the **GIFT** of God--16 and in one body to reconcile both of them to God through the **CROSS**, by which he put to death their hostility.*

The **KING OF KINGS, JESUS CHRIST the MESSIAH** showed me how fairy tales and things of the imagination can be used to promote the agenda of the darkness, the spirit of the world. God's ways are built on a foundation of **TRUTH** to help us build our **FAITH**. In a figurative sense Jesus is our **SUPERNATURAL step-father.** It was the first man Adam's blood that we **INHERITED** making him our first **NATURAL father.** My **stepfather** adopted me and my siblings to give us his surname, **CROSS.** [6]**Surname** according to Webster's dictionary means the name **borne in common by members of a family.**" [6]*Merriam-Webster.com* My first thought was, as believers in Christ, we are called Christians because surname means the name we all have in common. **WE WERE PREDESTINED FOR ADOPTION TO SONSHIP THROUGH JESUS CHRIST BY WAY OF THE CROSS.**

*[Ephesians 1:5 NIV] 5 he **predestined us for ADOPTION to sonship through Jesus Christ,** in accordance with His pleasure and will--*

Getting To Know My Heavenly Father

Hence, as God's children we all have a **CROSS** to bear. The crossbearer is the KING of ISRAEL. Compare *John 1:49-51* and *Isaiah 44:5* We share the surname of Israel as Christians whether Jew or Gentiles grafted in.

*[Isaiah 44:5 KJV] 5 One shall say, I [am] the LORD'S; and another shall call [himself] by the name of Jacob; and another shall subscribe [with] his hand unto the LORD, and **surname [himself] by the name of Israel.***

[John 1:49-50 NIV] *49 Then Nathanael declared, "Rabbi, you are the Son of God; you are the king of Israel." 50 Jesus said, "You believe because I told you I saw you under the fig tree. You will see greater things than that."*

Christ is called the **(LAST)** Adam, our EVERLASTING **FATHER** replacing the **FIRST** Adam. Not only have we inherited the **name of Israel** but a **new life** and a **new spirit**. Glory to God! I never had a close relationship with my real father or stepfather, but I wanted to. I longed to have that Father and daughter bond that many people are blessed to have in their lives. *1Cor 15:45, Luke 14:27*

[Romans 8:15 NIV] *15 The Spirit you received does not make you slaves, so that you live in fear again; rather, the Spirit you received brought about* **your ADOPTION to sonship.** *And by Him we cry,* **"Abba, Father** *."* ...

[Isaiah 9:6 NIV] *6 For to us a child is born, to us a son is given, and the government will be on His shoulders. And* **He will be called** *Wonderful Counselor, Mighty God,* **Everlasting Father,** *Prince of Peace.*

Rejection is what I felt from my real father. He would come and pick me up when I was a little girl for holidays like Easter or to buy me clothes for my first days of school. But I don't remember him ever hugging me, picking me up, or telling me that he loved me. If he did I'm sure I would remember it. We lost contact with each other for many years. When I was in my early twenties I somehow got a hold of his address. I remember him coming to the door holding it closed behind him. He never invited me in or invited me to come back if that was not a good time. It felt rather awkward. It hurt me deeply.

But God! He knew how much I longed for the love of a Father. He has been the most loving, and caring Father in my life. Through Jesus the Father revealed Himself to me in ways I can't fully explain. At times in my spirit I knew it was the Father's love I was feeling. It felt as though He were holding and hugging me. I could sense feeling His welcoming smile when I'd go before the throne of **GRACE.** He lives inside of each believer's heart and when you connect with Him in that special place inside it brings **JOY** and **PEACE.** Peace that surpasses all understanding. The Father has revealed sacred things to me concerning who He is, especially related to His name. I hope you get to know Him like that. Jesus is amazing. He's grace wrapped up in the person of our Father. He's directing all the steps in **MY** dance with Him. In your dance, are you following His lead into the light of grace and truth? What I appreciate most is how the Father demonstrated His love through giving us His only begotten Son to die for us. What a loving sacrifice for us sinners. Jesus is the way, the truth and the life. *John 14:6* Are you enjoying your life through your dance with **GRACE**?

> *I danced with **GRACE**, to feel the*
> ***Father's love** in **Jesus EMBRACE***

[John 1:17 KJV] *17 For the law was given by Moses, [but]* **grace and truth** *came by Jesus Christ.*

[Col 1:6 KJV] 6 *Which is come unto you, as [it is] in all the world; and bringeth forth fruit, as [it doth] also in you,.. ye heard [of it], and* **knew the grace of God in truth:**

[2 John 1:3 KJV] 3 **Grace be with you, mercy, [and] peace, from God the Father,** *and from the Lord Jesus Christ, the Son of the Father, in truth and love.*

Pondering, I wondered about how my step-father gave me his last name but didn't do it through the court system. Here's another object lesson! In our metaphor, we all receive Christ's new name. Yes, legally the spiritual name change takes place in the divine **COURTS** of **HEAVEN,** not here in the earthly court system. Glory to God!!!! Wow That makes perfect sense to me because we know that our names are registered in the **Lamb's BOOK OF LIFE.** Best of all, the blood of the Lamb brought about our reconciliation with Abba Father. Amen!!! *Colossians 1:20 John 3:16*

*[Rev 3:11-12 KJV] 11 Behold, I come quickly: hold that fast which thou hast, that no man take thy crown. ….…..: and I will write upon him the name of my God, and the name of the city of my God, [which is] new Jerusalem, ...[**I will write upon him] my new name***

Gifts From The Father Of Grace

I've discovered that the Lord brings everything together in His own timing. Sometime in the early part of 2017 the Lord led me to start looking for a new apartment. I had been living in my apartment for 8 years and now the Lord said it was time for me to move.

I looked at several apartments online while seeking more direction from the Lord. My thinking was that the Lord wanted me to move to another state. So, I discovered that my apartment management had a lovely apartment building in Mt. Vernon, Illinois not too far from my hometown.

Going back home to visit family and friends would only be an hour or so away. I went one day to see the apartment and was pleased with what I saw. The apartments were called **Heritage Landing** and was it by chance the apartment I was shown faced a beautifully landscaped area where the office manager showing me around said deer often grazed. Was God saying, this is a small glimpse of what your heritage landing of paradise will look like?

I love countryside living and that's exactly what it reminded me of. It's how I imagine my surroundings of my heavenly mansion to be like. It was astounding to find out the city had the royal nickname **"KING CITY"** dating back to **1888**. I had no clue about this until I got home and did some research on the town. Though I loved the apartment, it was perfect in almost every way but there was only **ONE thing** I didn't like. It was a small thing yet I couldn't get past it. The **lights** in the hallway were extremely **dim**, making the hallways too **dark**. It was around 12 noon and yet it looked and felt like evening or night time because there were no windows in the hallway.

Dimmed lights would be appropriate for a romantic atmosphere, but if I'm coming home to my apartment at any given time of the day or night, I'm not looking for any romantic connections in the hallway. I prefer lighted hallways over dark ones for obvious reasons. (smiling)

[John 8:12 NKJV] 12 Then Jesus spoke to them .., saying, **"I am the light of the world. He who follows Me shall not walk in darkness**, but have the **light of life**."

[John 11:9 NKJV] 9 Jesus answered, "Are there not twelve hours in the day? If anyone **walks in the day, he does not stumble**, because he sees the light of this world.

The lights were designed to make the lights dim, casting a dark shadow in the hallway, so it seemed to me and I found this to be odd. I thought, why would they make it so dark in the hallways? Maybe they thought bright lights would be too much for the elderly people's eyes, I don't know. Anyways, I decided it was not the apartment for me, at least for the time being. I felt led to look elsewhere. The few apartments I liked had long waiting lists and my lease was due to expire in a few months. For that reason, I was really getting anxious because I wanted to move, it was time to go. If I didn't find anything by my deadline, I would be forced to sign a new one year lease.

Time was quickly passing. It seemed out of nowhere I learned about an apartment not far from where I was already living that was available.

I went to see the apartment and knew right away the Lord wanted me to move there. The apartment building resembles a rustic chateau-like white stone fortress, on a beautifully landscaped lot with lots of mature trees lining a walking trail. Having found what looked to be God's choice for me, I realized I hadn't fully counted the cost of moving. I soon realized I didn't have the necessary funds to move.

I would need money for a moving truck and movers, a deposit and first month's rent and other associated expenses. I'm retired on a budget. So, I prayed to the Lord with my lease now only a few weeks from expiring and I had given my notice to move even though I didn't have the money yet. I told the Lord in prayer, Lord, if this is your will for me to move which I believe it is, please make a way for me to get the money. Otherwise if it's not your will I will trust you. I will accept the fact it's not your will if you don't make a way for me to get the money I need. I left everything in His hands.

One day soon after that prayer I opened a **JAW DROPPING** piece of mail that had a real check in it for the exact amount of money I would need to move with some extra to buy a few new items for my new apartment. This was indeed going to be a **NEW BEGINNING** for me after **8 years** in my old apartment. The apartments were beautifully renovated. I like seeing old things become new. I can see a metaphor in almost anything and I saw myself in my newly renovated apartment for a time such as this.

I thought about how once we receive our glorified bodies, it will be a **total makeover and renovation but better.** I started shouting and praising the Lord as He showed me that this was His will for me to move there. His perfect timing gave me the opportunity to choose from the best apts available. In my eyes, I got the perfect view overlooking the courtyard and chapel with a beautiful pink magnolia tree and oak trees in clear view of my windows.

Everyday I get to watch the adorable squirrels and colorful birds playing in the trees which bring me so much joy. When we get to the real **King's City,** heaven's **New Jerusalem,** there we will have our heart's desires fulfilled in the fullest sense. Beautiful mansions designed by the Lord to suit our personal taste.

*[John 14:2-3 KJV] 2 In my Father's house are **many mansions**: if [it were] not [so], I would have told you. I go to prepare a place for you. 3 And if I go and prepare a place for you, I will come again, and receive you unto myself; that where I am, [there] ye may be also.*

I have always loved watching the squirrels play while admiring nature, especially flowers and trees, so... this was a **GIFT** I had not been praying for or expecting. Those are the best kind of gifts, aren't they? I discerned that God wanted to move me into a bigger space so I could feel more comfortable and relaxed. The relaxing atmosphere would make it easier to work on my music and books for **My Dance with the King of King's** projects.

I was grateful for my old apartment in spite of my view being the parking lot. (smiling) My apt was small but cute and I never complained to the Lord about it. But, I had been undergoing many severe trials and testing of spiritual warfare in that place. Although the Lord moved me to a new place reflecting His **BEAUTY, GRACE, FAVOR and MERCY,** I would have to contend with the same strongholds and even worse at my new apartment. As they say, new level, new devils. We can't get away from it. No matter where we live, this world is covered by a dense spiritual darkness.

I learned we have to deal with our issues and face our demons with the help of the Lord wherever we live. Also, I have to say the place I moved from was beautiful and still is a nice place to live, it was just God's will and timing for me to move. Astonishingly, the check was more than I would have ever expected to receive in the mail. The timing reminded me that the Lord's name is a mighty strong **tower** and into it the righteous run. I had prayed to my Lord for a specific need and he answered me by providing what I needed plus more. *Prov 18:10* He moved me into a place where the outside appearance again reminds me of HIM being a **MIGHTY STRONG TOWER** and **FORTRESS**. God is not a respecter of persons, for this is every Christian's **HERITAGE LANDING**.

*[PROVERBS 18:10] 10 The **name of the LORD** [is] **a strong tower**: the righteous runneth into it, and are safe.*

We are called to be warriors for God's kingdom and He provides all the weapons of warfare for the battle. The common theme if you'll notice was God showing me how He's a **MIGHTY** God full of strength and power. God's gift of **GRACE** is what I'm talking about. Glory to God. He also provides the angelic hosts to help us with the separating work as reapers of the **HARVEST** as we encounter people walking along the Broadway of life. Compare *Ephesians 6:11-17*

*[Isaiah 35:8-10 NKJV] 8 A highway shall be there, and a road, And it shall be called the **Highway of Holiness**. The unclean shall not pass over it, But it [shall be] for others. Whoever walks the road, although a fool, Shall not go astray.*

*9 No lion shall be there, Nor shall [any] ravenous beast go up on it; It shall not be found there. But the **redeemed shall walk [there]**, 10 And the **ransomed of the LORD** shall return, And come to **Zion with singing, With everlasting joy on their heads. They shall obtain joy and gladness, And sorrow and sighing shall flee away.***

GRACE BY WAY OF THE CROSS

Amazing Grace will lead us in the way of righteousness. Oh, how sweet that sounds! The Lord is graciously teaching each one of us through these object lessons how much he **LOVES us.** When we seek first the kingdom, all other things we need will be added. *Matt 6:33* It's not by chance that He would first lead me to see a view of our heritage, at the **HERITAGE LANDING** apts in Mt. Vernon aka **KING CITY.** *It was like the Lord giving me a glimpse of the new earth under Christ's millennial reign.* I was shown apt **#307 on the third floor. 3** and **7** speak of God's **deity** and **perfection**. It reminds us of God's heavenly kingdom in the **third heavens, New Jerusalem which makes the perfect New Heavens and Earth possible, a prepared place by Jesus.**

The dark hallway was a reminder that all creation is subjected to a fallen world (earth) at the present time. The property (earth) is temporarily under the dominion of the spiritually dark hostile forces, God's enemies. In spite of this I was reminded as I looked at the beautiful landscape out that apartment window that God's kingdom will come here on earth as it is now in heaven someday soon. Yes, someday soon, but not our idea of soon. He will bring to realization His original plan for the earth, **restoring all things** through the hands of His **Chosen HOLY One..** *Psalm 89:13-23*

The beautiful landscape and grazing deer reminded me of the bible's poetic language referencing the beauty, power, and strength of the **MAJESTIC ONE,** the **KING OF KINGS.** He stands at the threshold of destiny as the prophetic **Joshua, (Yehoshua) YESHUA (Jesus Christ)** our **Warrior King**. Yet, He is as graceful and beautiful as a deer grazing among the wheat fields ready for harvesting, or likened to the lilies of the field. In His own timing, the Lord will **LEAD** the saints in taking over the land which is the promised inheritance for Abraham's offspring, Israel. Yes, their **HERITAGE.** Before we cross over into the promised land, we must face the hostile enemy forces. *Song 2:8-10* It bears repeating, the dark hallway reminded me that we are living in a time of dense spiritual darkness that covers the land which calls for spiritual warfare. For privacy I can't say the name of my new apartment complex or its location but the name of the apartments actually mean **"army, warriors and warfare". Could all of this be by chance or accident.** I must say, as I've had time to think about all of this, it's not surprising. How's that? Because...remember...

The Lord is writing all the details of this narrative, He is the AUTHOR and FINISHER of our FAITH.

*[Heb 12:2 KJV] 2 Looking unto Jesus the **author and finisher of [our] faith**; who for the joy that was set before him endured the cross, despising the shame, and is set down at the right hand of the throne of God.*

He's speaking to all those who have ears to hear what the Spirit is saying today. The Lord reminds me that through Him we have **DIVINE AUTHORITY** to overcome the enemy because we're seated with Him in heavenly places, the city of New Jerusalem. *Luke 10:19,20* By faith we can go before the throne of grace and ask God for whatever we need to be victorious in our battle. We're assured by God that His eyes are on all those who belong to **HIM**. That means grace sometimes answers before we ask. Noah was said to have found **GRACE** in the **EYES** of the **LORD.** *Gen 6:8* Perhaps, we're about to move into a new dispensation as we take note of our calling as the **overcomers,** the true sons of God manifesting the glory. We've each been drafted to fight in a spiritual war as a part of God's army, the nation of Israel whether we are natural branches or grafted in. The key is remembering the weapons of our warfare are not carnal but **MIGHTY through GOD**. I can't say that too many times because our refuge is in GOD alone, not in our puny flesh. He'll fight every battle for us as He did for Joshua and Moses if we look to the strong tower He is and take refuge in Him. Compare *Prov 18:10 2Cor 10:3-5 Psalm 34:15*

[2Cor 10: 3-5 KJV] 3 "For though we walk in the flesh, we do not war after the flesh; 4 (For the weapons of our warfare are not carnal, mighty through God to the pulling down of strong holds;) 5 Casting down imaginations, and every high thing that exalteth itself against the knowledge of God, and bringing into captivity every thought to the obedience of Christ."

I understand this time to be not only a time of personal spiritual battles but a time to share in the ingathering of the great harvest. There is much work to be done along the way to share the good news of the kingdom with the poor, the outcast and those naturally overlooked like the homeless and depressed. Sadly, the focus is mainly the pursuit of worldly interest. The true remnant church has gladly accepted Christ's invitation to the wedding feast by putting God's Kingdom agenda in first place. We warn the wicked of His coming wrath, while going out to the **highways and byways to invite those considered the least into the kingdom and the wedding feast**.

I find joy in letting them know they don't have to face God's wrath but face His face of Grace, the Father's mercy. *Compare Matthew 22:8-9* God has shown us through object lessons not only **WHO** He is in **Jesus Christ (Yeshua Ha Maschiah)** as Messiah but also **WHO** He is in **believers.**

Jesus is our **GPS!** Our **GUIDE PROTECTOR SAVIOUR**, the **GLORIOUS POWER SOURCE** of **GOD'S PRECIOUS SPIRIT**. We serve a God who is a **GENEROUS PROVISIONS SUPPLIER**. His favor, the power of love and compassion removes all obstacles in the way of His will and purpose being a God of His Word. It's all about **HIM. Amazing Grace!!!!!!!** When we see the person of **GRACE PURPOSE SERVED** through Christ's direction, we find peace and fulfillment in the dance of grace.

Considering everything, it's clear to see the Lord does indeed order our steps. He gave me a name to challenge me to live up to the things I would most appreciate and come to write about. Those things were **FAITH, GRACE**, and the **CROSS**. His patient, loving hand continues to guide me to step in line with Him through the darkness and storms centered around the **"CROSS"** that I would have to bear and continue to bear. He that endures to the end shall be saved. *Matt 24:13*

I danced with *GRACE, to see the Father's MERCY on Jesus FACE*

Dancing with the King of Kings at its best is the most **"GRACE"**ful synchronized dance which is preordained, choreographed and purposefully directed by the Lord Himself through Holy Spirit. Every dance step doesn't always feel or appear to be done with ease or perfection. It is only by the **GRACE** of God that we can get back in step when we make a wrong move. Everyone has a unique dance with Him as He leads and directs us to bear our **CROSS**. We move by His grace and mercy towards the cross of crucifixion everyday. By way of the cross, do you see the Lord as the **CENTERPIECE** of your life? Or, are we only concerned about what God can do for us? Have we learned to put God's will and purpose before our own selfish desires. Everyone has a special calling for something that requires dedication and sacrifice.

It could be something for your family, your community, country, or for the world. Think of something you have a passion for or a special talent or gift you've been blessed with. In any case, whatever he's called you to do, it will require His grace which lends to Him getting all the glory. HalleluYAH! I appreciate the **grace and mercy** shown me down through the years to the extent of the call God put on my life. No one is less deserving of the ministry and spiritual gifts He has given me than me. When I look at myself through my flesh, under no circumstances will I ever feel secure or qualified for the writing of any book or producing a music CD. Everyday I'm reminded that I am far from perfect and fall short of His glory. I can't boast about anything about myself. I'm no better than the next person. I have often fallen into sexual sin, lied, cheated others by stealing their money and worse. But God, is all I can say. Thank you for your grace and mercy Father. *Psalm 103:4-6, 8*

I'm reminded that I graduated at the very bottom of my high school class of nearly 400 students. That's pretty bad. For much of my adult life I tried to forget about that but it would always somehow creep back into my mind. Often I heard myself saying at times, Faye you are so dumb. You graduated at the bottom of your class'. I hated school because I was often bullied, causing me to always feel left out and awkward around people in any setting. You would find me always in the corner sulking by myself as I was made to feel unworthy.

Everybody else always seemed to be better and smarter than me. In spite of all that, I know and trust the Lord is doing the work through me because I'm a willing vessel to be used by Him. He chose me for this work, I didn't choose myself. He's doing all the work through me as I avail myself to the calling. Because of His unconditional love, I have learned to see my self worth in **HIM** alone. I give him **ALL** the **GLORY** and rejoice in knowing He loves me in spite of myself. As the tears fall now thinking about how gracious and merciful God has been to me, I will be forever grateful to Him. Never desire what God has given someone else. Be content with being who God made you to be. One thing I've learned is to like who God created me to be. I can't sing like Yolanda Adams or Jennifer Hudson who both have powerful voices. I sing to express my love for God which He put in my heart to share with others. *Psalm 119:77 Hebrews 13:5*

It's Not A Competition, Just Do It For God

My voice is not forceful or strong, my voice often cracks or squeaks out of tune but I sing the way the Lord created me to sing. I say this to help someone who's feeling called to sing but lacks the confidence because someone laughed at you. One person told me when she first heard me sing, she laughed saying who is this lady singing with a funny sounding voice. I'll never forget that because I've heard her say it at least twice.

But I knew to be me and be content with what I've been given by God. I never asked God to give me a voice like Yolanda Adams or Jennifer Hudson. I only knew I was being given songs that I wanted to share with everyone I could in little small settings and one on one. Compare *Gal 5:14-15, 26 6:2-5* I'm naturally shy and still don't understand why God put me in this position but I don't want to continue to question God's choosing me for this calling. I'm learning to accept it and be grateful. I do it for Him. This way He gets the GLORY!

[1 Corinthians 1:26-31 NIV] 26 Brothers and sisters, think of what you were when you were called. **Not many of you were wise by human standards**; *not many were influential; not many were of noble birth. 27 But God chose the foolish things of the world to shame the wise; God chose the weak things of the world to shame the strong. 28 God chose the lowly things of this world and the despised things..., 29 so that* **no one may boast** *before him. 30 It is because of him that you are in Christ Jesus, who has become for us wisdom from God--that is, our righteousness, holiness and redemption. 31 Therefore, as it is written:* **"Let the one who boasts boast in the Lord."**

As you continue to read my *"Dance with the King of Kings"* you will understand how it was and will always be my *"FAITH"* in the Lord that had to be developed. I was **TRIED** and **TESTED** by **GREAT** measure along the way, in my journey through my dance. It is my hope you will appreciate seeing more of my journey through my journal timeline. It paints a vivid picture of the many missteps I made as the Lord and I danced together. We're all justified by faith. *Gal 3:26*

[Gal 3:26 KJV] For ye are all the children of God by faith in Christ Jesus.

Everyone has a special purpose. It is up to us individually to find out what it is, and submit fully to the call. Only then can we find true peace and contentment in this life.

In your song and dance I hope you see yourself as Christ does, He loves us all. He died for the world, not for a few individuals. However, it's true only a remnant will follow Him onto the narrow road, the only way to eternal life. Jesus is the only way. *Matt 7:13-14 Rom 8:28 and John 11:52*

Relax and Enjoy Your Dance

There's a wonderful place of His sabbath rest that I've found in the Lord **Jesus(Yeshua)**, the King of Glory and my Abba Father **Yahweh(Jehovah)** that is quite refreshing. Since writing about my sabbath rest in the Lord, the enemy has come along to challenge me in my **FAITH** and relationship with Him. But we must remain steadfast, unmovable keeping on our suit of armor, especially holding on to our shield of faith. *Mark 13:13* Even though I can't see Him I know He's with me each and every moment of the day and night.

Even when I can't hear Him or feel His presence, I just know that I know because I trust Him. Our dance is all about trust which comes out of **FAITH**. Can you think back at any given time when you were dancing with a partner and you wanted to lead instead of follow? I remember one such experience.

I would either trip over his feet or just go too fast or too slow because I didn't fully trust his leading me. If I would have relaxed and let him lead we would have been dancing in unison. Instead we were dancing totally out of sync. That's sort of how it is with our first dance with the King, at least mine. We begin not knowing how to dance with Him. We have to allow Him to take the lead and simply trust and enjoy the dance. Dancing with the Lord is like communicating with the Lord through prayer, worship, study time, reading, meditating on the Word and soaking in His presence.

If we're not communing with the Lord in any way, everything else breaks down. We're no longer dancing in sync. *Psalm 43:3, 143:10* When we are close to the Lord, seeking His will, we don't always have to think about His next move. He lets us know sometimes because He tells us. I was blessed one day about twelve years ago. While in line at the grocery store, a total stranger standing in front of me looked me in the eye and said the Lord had given her a message for me. I was startled, no one had ever approached me in this way nor since.

She told me I would someday have a ministry, that God would use me more than I realized to minister to others. She also told me that she knew about my issues with managing anger but she assured me that God would help me to overcome it. I've come a long way since that day seeing how He has given me a ministry to minister in several different ways.

The anger problem, well let's just say I'm still a work in progress. (smiling) Just when I thought it was all under control, I was tested and failed horribly. I said all of that to say, when we discover the Lord's calling on our life, and we embrace it, it brings comfort to dance with our King. He will never turn away or give up on us. Yes, never give up on yourself.

During the dance He can tell us the details of how we are to go about the Father's business. Then we can anticipate moves or just trust Him when we don't know what to do next. So the best thing is to simply follow His lead. He may add a fancy turn just to add depth and enrichment to our experience as we get better dancing together. As the dance gets smoother we can relax enjoying our time just resting our head on His shoulder following His lead. The key is being focused on HIM and the things of heaven that await us. At times however, distractions come by way of trials to distract us. The **JOY** set before us helps to keep us in the race only because we were His **JOY that was set before Him** which motivated Him to endure a torture stake. He loves you and I so much beloved.

Bearing My Cross With Grace And Mercy

Yes, for sure not everything will be hunky dory. As a matter of fact it's in the times of the hardest trials that we can rest our head on His shoulder and allow Him to lead us in the dance of grace. When times get tough, we can't give up even if we want to. I've had my crosses to bear like everyone else. Some things we have to accept and put up with because either it can't be changed or God refuses to change it in spite of our asking Him to, or it's just not the right time. Everyone's lost loved ones which can be one of our heaviest crosses to bear. I will tell you a bit later about some of these heavy crosses of losing loved ones. I've had my share of health issues with depression and anxiety brought on for various reasons. I know what it's like to want to commit suicide. At one point I swallowed a handful of sedatives, only crying for help.

Too many times I've been in pain in my body from arthritis to the point I couldn't lift my legs or feet to even tie my shoe strings. Pain so bad the only thing I could do was cry in agony praying for relief. Often I've gone to the emergency room being in pain or with health scares concerning my heart. But God is all I can say. The pain in different parts of my body is something I learned to endure and continue to pray about. The Lord many times has answered my prayers for healing in my body taking away the pain. During these health challenges I learned to eat better and take better care of my body.

Another cross for me to bear has been me not having ever married or have children. I had several opportunities to get married, getting engaged three times. But I decided I didn't want to marry, I just didn't feel like I was cut out for it.

I knew I was selfish and liked having my freedom to come and go and do as I pleased. Yet on cold nights being alone can be a challenge when you wish you had someone to snuggle up with or watch a movie with. The enemy likes to taunt us at these vulnerable moments which only makes matters worse. I especially regret not having children because now that I'm in the winter season of my life I have no children to look after me or grandchildren to call me nanna or granny. (smiling)

No grandchildren to stay overnight that I can spoil with lots of gifts and presents and hugs and kisses. My cross to bear is me knowing that if I hadn't had an abortion when I was 23 yrs young, I could possibly have had at least one son or daughter with some grandchildren now. But the good news is, I will have at least one son or daughter waiting for me in heaven. In spite of my crosses to bear, I wouldn't trade my life for any other. My Lord has filled the empty places in my heart with His love. I love the fact that I can devote all my time and attention to Him without distractions most of the time. I love the ministries He's given me to occupy my time in my years of retirement. But yes, no doubt it does get hard so we must all pray to endure to the end, to the end of our life or when the Lord returns for His bride church.

A Proven Roadmap To Treasure

I believe there is available to everyone a roadmap to the Lord's **HEART.** And though the **law of LOVE** has been inscribed on each Christian's heart, not everyone will open their heart to find it. Those who truly love God will find that this treasure map is worth seeking out because He's the **TREASURE.** *Job 22:25* I found Him and you too can find Him inside of your heart if you haven't discovered Him there yet. When you really want something you keep looking and searching for it as if it were some hidden treasure waiting to be discovered. You will appreciate it when you enter that special place with Him. *Compare Isaiah 33:6 and Matthew 13:45* The more I read the Word of God, the more I wanted to learn and understand what God wanted of me. Without knowing it, I was hiding the Word inside of my heart. The more we seek His presence, the easier it is to hear His still small voice. It draws us closer and closer to cherish each dance encounter. Glory!!!!!

On the treasure map we will find there are **clues** and **helpful hints** to lead us to Him. It tells us how to get from point **A** to point **B**. It tells you and I what pleases and displeases Him. One sure way of getting to Him is through what I call the **seven P's** which I have listed below.

(P)ath, (P)oint, (P)lease, (P)ress (P)rayer, (P)raise and (P)ure

We must follow the **P**ath God has called us to, wherever the Spirit of the Lord **P**oints us; be motivated by love, having a desire to **P**lease Him in every way and the fear to dis**p**lease Him in any way. In all of this it will require that we **P**ress into Him through **P**rayer, **P**raise and **P**ure **worship** which means to worship Him in **spirit** and **truth**. *Read John 4: 23-24* If we can **p**ut these **p**ositive **p**rinciples into **p**ractice among other **p**rinciples they will bring all the **p**lans and **p**urposes of God for our life into **p**lace. Hallelu**YAH**! Glory to God!!! *Compare 2 Peter 1:2-10 Job 28:28 Proverbs 3:5*

[Proverbs 19:23 KJV] *23 The fear of the LORD [tendeth] to life: and [he that hath it] shall abide satisfied; he shall not be visited with evil.*

[Proverbs 22:4 KJV] *4 By humility [and] the fear of the LORD [are] riches, and honour, and life.*

A NEW BEGINNING

There's a saying, one path leads to another path. I will never forget, in **November 2008** on a Sunday morning, I answered an altar call at church. The call was for those who wanted to come up for prayer, to receive a blessing with anointed oil. This was the first time ever I'd been blessed with anointing oil by anyone. I took a deep breath, got up from my seat and walked slowly up to the front to the brother holding the bottle of oil in his hands. I answered the Lord calling me to repentance as I followed the leading of His voice. I'm reminded of *James 5:14,*

"Is anyone among you sick? He should call for the elders of the church, and they should **pray over him after anointing him with olive oil in the name of the Lord.***" HCSB*

At this time of my life I was a fornicator, at a dead end, and crossroad in my life. I was a lousy dancer at this point having taken the lead but I was willing now to let Him guide me by taking back the lead in our dance. One major dance step I had to follow was the Lord moving me back to my hometown in Missouri. I say this because for several years it seemed I could not find a job where I felt comfortable. Unaware, for years I ran from the Lord. Now unemployed, a few months away from being evicted from my apartment, I was in a toxic relationship, depressed, feeling lost and confused.

I had moved to the state of Texas in 1994 to serve where the need was great. I went to help out with a newly established Spanish speaking congregation in a small rural town about 90 miles east of Dallas, Texas. I left a good job, family and friends behind. Fast forward 14 years in 2008, having gone back to the world, I was in deep mud. My spiritual compass pointed me in God's direction as I sought to get back on track, after losing my way somehow.

Learning God's Anointing Is Real

So, when I got home from church that memorable day I laid down to take a nap. But the Lord would not let me sleep. He awakened my spirit with a song in my heart to the melody of Burt Bacharach's song **"Alfie"**. Do you remember that song? I loved it! This was the first of several **LOVE** songs I would go on to write to the Lord. After that day he began to not only give me lyrics for songs but original melodies I could call my own though I give Him all the glory, honor and praise for every song I've written. But going back to the song **"Alfie"**, Dionne Warwick made this song popular back in the 60's and she starts off singing, asking a question. *'What's it all about Alfie?'* But I heard in my spirit, *'What's it all about, Jesus?'*

I continued singing the lyrics the Lord had put in my heart *'Life has no meaning without youuuuu ooh ooh And what's life all about Jesus?'* It sounded as beautiful as Dionne's **"Alfie"**, with better lyrics surely because I was singing it to the Lord.

Blessed With The Gift Of Songwriting

This was the beginning of my journey of songwriting for the Lord. My prayer is that one day I may get permission to make a recording of those lyrics the Lord gave me that day to the melody of Alfie. I believe many of the melodies of Burt Bacharach and the Bee Gees with Barry Gibb and brothers are melodies straight from heaven. I've written many beautiful lyrics to several of the Gibb brothers' song melodies that I also hope to one day record or someone else record if I could ever get their permission. I wrote the vision down on paper so it's in the Master's hand. If anyone can make it happen, He can if it's His will. In October 2009, I wrote my first song that falls under the category of a wedding song for the bridegroom and bride church, called **"It's a Love Made in Heaven"**. I had no idea back then it would be the beginning of a theme I would develop for a music CD and an accompanying book. I later wrote another song which was about heaven, speaking of our real home called **"New Jerusalem"** in 2011, 2 yrs later. I suppose God's timing is everything.

***Psalm 37:23** says, "The steps of a [good] man **(or woman)** are ordered by the LORD, And He delights in his way." NKJV*

He would give me other love songs every now and then but most of the early songs I wrote were about the heartache, pain, trial and tribulation that I had experienced over the years. It's been within the last few years of 2015-2017 the Lord drew my attention to the actual wedding celebration that the bible calls the wedding supper of the Lamb. Somewhere around 2014-2015 he gave me the vision for the book and CD **"Dancing with the King of Kings"**.

Helped By An Angel

I hope you don't mind me digressing here to go back to what was happening with me in Texas. A month had passed since the altar call and the Lord was really dealing with me. It was in December 2008, I found myself selling most of my possessions after getting my eviction notice. I was willing to go to a shelter if I became homeless. I had done my research to find out which shelter would be the best for me. Finding a shelter that offered a place to sleep at night and job training during the day was what I searched for and found. I didn't know if they had any beds available or not because I never got to that point of going to the shelter.

The Lord at the last minute provided me with the necessary funds to move ahead in another direction which was moving back home. I chose to follow His direction by going back home. The Lord finally got His way leading me back to St. Louis. It's Jan 2009 and everything began to fall into place for me after moving back to the city where I was born and raised. This was a fast dance with the King but I kept up with Him. Things had happened quickly in succession after my altar call at church.

Back home in Missouri the show me state, one of my sisters opened up her home to me. She showed me that sisterly love which gave me time to rest on the Lord's shoulder as we danced. I will always be grateful to her for giving me a place to stay. It's amazing how our dance steps are dependent on how connected we are to the spirit of Jesus inside of us. After three months I had found a full-time job affording me the opportunity to get my own place again. Through this time of testing, I learned to know when we're in or out of the will of God. It took me a while to recognize the strong signal God had been sending me when nothing seemed to work. True repentance required me to move, leaving my adulterous affair behind. That was the case for me before moving back to St. Louis. I felt totally out of sync and out of step with the Lord. It was because I was not where the Lord wanted me to be.

No job seemed to feel right though it may have paid the bills at the time. If we continue doing things our own way, ignoring God's prodding, He will take away the job and everything else that's standing in the way. Then you know it's time to seek the Lord's direction as I did. Once I repented of my sinful lifestyle, where God wanted me, He blessed me by providing me with everything I needed at the time. Further, He replaced things I had lost. This brings to mind a testimony I have to share here if I may speak of the goodness and favor of the Lord. I had the money to move and get settled in St. Louis when I returned home because God put it in the heart of a stranger to give me some money. It was not in the sense that I met him on the street. In the last week of December 2008, I was about to be evicted. I was grasping for straws, trying to stay in Texas. I went to a charitable agency similar to the Salvation Army as my last hope to get some help to pay my rent. When I walked in, there was a room full of people but I went ahead and signed the book at the receptionist desk. People were steadily coming in as I sat there patiently waiting to be called.

I didn't know what they would be able to do for me but I was hopeful to at least get some help with utilities or a food voucher. Every little bit would help at this point. I sat there watching people get called and from the expressions on their faces I could tell they were not getting what they had hoped for. I overheard several conversations that basically went like this, 'I'm sorry but we are out of funds at this time but here is a bag for you to take home a few grocery items from our food pantry'. My heart sank as I heard this over and over.

But through it all I sat there praying silently asking the Lord to help me. After sitting there for more than two hours I began noticing people that came in after me were getting called. I walked up to the receptionist desk to inquire and somewhat complain. Shortly afterwards, this middle aged man walked over to me, as I was practically the last person left in the building. I'll never forget, there was something different about this man that I discerned right away. I didn't know what it was until later. I'll never forget he told me he saw chains and darkness around me but assured me that the Lord would set me free. He took me over to another area asking how he could help. We have groceries in our pantry for you, he said. How else can we help you?' I told him about my utility bill and my back rent. I'm so sorry, we can't help you in those regards. We're out of funds being stretched during this holiday season. He said, excuse me for a minute, I'll go get your groceries from the pantry. He came back with two large brown bags of groceries for which I was grateful for. He extended his hand and as he shook my hand I felt him putting something inside of my hand. I looked and saw he had put six new crisp one hundred dollar bills in my hand. Glory to God!

This was truly a gift from God. I stood there stunned and speechless. He told me that he knew I was a sister in Christ and that the Lord had told him to bless me. This was the reason why he had me wait around. By now, I was the only person left in the building, but I didn't feel threatened in any way. As a matter of fact the gentleman had an angelic persona or aura about himself. Praise God! I'm convinced God sent me to meet one of His angels working here on the earth. I give thanks, praise and honor to God for His love and mercy that endures forever into all eternity. Praise Yah!!!

[Psalm 118:28-29] *"Thou [art] my God, and I will praise thee: [thou art] my God, I will exalt thee. 29 O give thanks unto the LORD; for [he is] good: for his mercy [endureth] for ever". KJV*

Finding My Way Back Home

As God ordered my steps, He provided everything I needed to accomplish His will. He made a way for me to take care of my elderly aunt, moving me less than five minutes from her home. Because my work schedule was flexible, I could devote most of my time to developing a new online devotional at the Lord's direction. I worked on the website for two years before I made it public. During this time I began writing other songs as well. The Lord provides whatever we need to accomplish the things He has called us to do. All we have to do is obey His voice and submit to His direction. During my last days in Texas I had heard an audible voice tell me not to go back to home.

The voice spoke two words directly in my ear. **'Don't go'**, the voice said. It was a loud, clear, distinct voice I had never heard before. I had been in Texas for fourteen years by this point in time. It was not an easy decision to leave Texas because in spite of everything I loved the weather and the culture among other things. After that many years I simply did not want to go back to St. Louis. I had made a few special friends though at this time I was feeling isolated and lonely having moved to Arlington, Texas away from my friends. But as I mentioned before I had been ignoring the voice of God telling me to return to St. Louis for some years. I believe the day I answered the altar call in Arlington, Texas and received the anointing of oil was a huge genuine milestone for me.

Ironically the name of the church was Faith Tabernacle. This was a day I stepped out in faith as I stood at the fork in the road of indecision. I didn't know which way to go. I didn't know how to anticipate His turns or moves yet but that's where faith and trust comes in. Wherever He was leading me I knew it was for my good. That's what time and experience can do for you. Somehow by now, I was beginning to discern the Lord's voice and know His presence after my anointed encounter at Faith Tabernacle. The audible voice I had heard in my ear saying **"don't go"** was **NOT** of God but of the enemy. The Lord's voice was clear within my spirit as I discerned it. You just know that you know when God is speaking.

I felt a deep conviction within my spirit that I had made the right decision to not listen to that audible voice. I could now hear the Lord in that still small voice say, turn around here, don't look back but look straight ahead, go this way Faye. I was now beginning to anticipate His every move. He had my attention and I was listening to His direction so I could follow Him down the right path. What helped was learning the seven, **"P" PRINCIPLES,** which put me on my way to victory. "Return home to your family", is what I heard in my spirit.

2008, was to be a new season of my life, a new beginning. Therefore, I made the decision to go back home and look after my aunt and assist one of my sisters who really needed me at the time. She had been caring for several family members since the time I went to Texas in 1994. In 2009, I began to take care of my aunt. I was her caretaker till she passed in 2013 at the age of 92.

[Isaiah 58:5, 7-8 HCSB] *5 Will the fast I choose be like this: A day for a person to deny himself, to bow his head like a reed, and to spread out sackcloth and ashes?* ***Will you call this a fast and a day acceptable to the LORD?*** *... 7* ***Is it not to share your bread with the hungry,*** *to bring the poor and homeless into your house, to clothe the naked when you see him, and* ***not to ignore your own flesh and blood?*** *8 Then your light will appear like the dawn, and* ***your recovery will come quickly.*** *Your righteousness will go before you, and the LORD's glory will be your rear guard.*

[Leviticus 25:10 NKJV] *10 'And you shall consecrate the fiftieth year, and proclaim liberty throughout [all] the land to all its inhabitants.* ***It shall be a Jubilee for you***; *and each of you shall return to his possession, and each of* ***you shall return to his family***.

I was blessed to have my aunt in my life for the time God allowed. She was always supportive and caring for me and my ministry work. While taking care of her, I learned from her example to be patient, caring, generous, merciful, kind and compassionate. These attributes did not come naturally to me. I was always a selfish, prideful arrogant person but the Lord would change me over the course of years. He's still working on me.

ON THE ROAD TO "DWTK" CD

The making of the **CD "Dancing with the King"** was in the making for many years. Starting from the beginning of my life when I was a little girl. As a little girl all through my grade school years through to high school, I always felt different and not a part of the crowd. I was a loner who at times tried to fit in with the in crowd. Being a loner, the Lord tells me it's not good for me. He's pushing me to be more sociable. Iron sharpens iron, he reminded me today as I'm writing this now.

At some point in time the Lord will lead us out to the wilderness to be alone with Him just as He was led out to the wilderness. It was all so I could learn from the great teacher. One day, He instructed me,

'Now I'm leading you back to start associating more with the other sheep around you in the pen. Though I led you to go off by yourself so that I could teach you one on one, it is time to move in closer to the other sheep. I'm still there with you.'

I was reminded of His promise, *"I will never leave you nor forsake you"*. *'You have much to share with them as I've taught you but there are many things you can and will learn from others as well my daughter',* He further said to me.

Many sheep will relate to the fact that I can say my heart was hurt as a child and even as an adult. So much so that the spirit of rejection was firmly planted inside of my heart and soul. I was often teased, bullied and made fun of in grade school because I went to school smelling of urine. I would wet the bed almost every night and go to school without bathing or clean underwear. Imagine the smell and you know children are brutally honest. At the time I was in a bubble of depression, lonely and filled with self hatred. I was around 9yrs old. Can you imagine, when I was in the fifth grade, they spread false rumors of me going with the school janitor because I would be polite to him. I was really hurt thinking everyone was believing these lies about me. I want you to understand clearly who I am and where I've come from. I want to be able to help anyone who may be reading this book who has gone through similar circumstances or knows someone who has.

My mother was only 16 yrs old when she had me. She was a teenager not knowing how to raise a child. In the beginning I was neglected but now I know she did her best. As she got older, she became a wonderful mother to me and I saw her as a good role model for me. She worked hard getting off of welfare to take care of me and all of my siblings. She became my best friend. Like most, I've lost loved ones. I lost my grandmother who was in her 90's when she died tragically in a house fire in our home.

The following year my mother who was my best friend died at the age of 39 unexpectedly when I was 20 yrs of age. At the time I was the oldest with five younger siblings, ages 19, 15, 9, 8 and 5. She died from a brain aneurysm. I became bitter and angry with God feeling he had taken our mother from us. My anger led me to neglect as well as mistreat my younger siblings, something I'm not proud of. A few years later one of my sisters committed suicide which I blamed myself for. Imagine all the anger, shame and guilt I felt. I tried to drown out all the pain... partying, sleeping around, dabbling in drugs and alcohol. How many of you can say you've been raped so many times it's embarrassing to give the total number of times. I'll tell you about a few. Once I was raped by a man who was 3 times my size, forcing me in the back seat of his cab. This was someone I thought I knew and could trust.

Another time I left with a stranger I met at a bar, who drove me 300 miles away from my home. Half way to Kansas City, I knew I had made a big mistake. We entered a hotel room and he violated me over and over. I was afraid to say anything after seeing the knife he laid on the table by the bed. I sat in total silence the whole drive there and back. Even as an adult in the workplace it seemed as though there was a target on my back that said, ATTACK her, she's insecure and vulnerable. So much so, in the workplace I was a victim of sexual harassment at one particular company I worked at.

They would call me on the inter-office phone and breathe heavily or make lewd sexual remarks. I actually knew the two guys that were doing it. One day they drew a sexually explicit picture of a man's private parts and laid it on my desk in my office. This is what I put up with back in the late 70's. I was too timid to confront the men who were sexually harassing me. Regrettably, I put up with it until I moved on to another company. Many women were like me who put up with this kind of treatment back in the 70's and 80's. The **ME TOO** movement has given women the moral support needed to confront sexual harassment and rape in the workplace. Some of you reading this will be thinking, oh you poor thing, but it was all part of **"My Dance with the King of Kings", my JESUS, the lover of my soul!!!** He was there in the classroom with me as I was being ridiculed, bullied, made fun of and talked about by my schoolmates. He was with me when I was being made fun of as an adult at different companies I worked at because I was emotionally and socially handicapped. He was there by my side when I was a victim of sexual harassment by two men I worked with on my job. He was in the back of the cab with me as I was raped and in the hotel room as I was raped at knife point. I could have been dead, killed so many times. But he has always protected me so I would be able to write this book about our dancing together. Perhaps you may be thinking, if God was with you why would He allow you to get into such dire predicaments. I can't say I know all the answers to why things happened but I got myself in some situations, by leaving a bar with a stranger all because I was looking for love in all the wrong places. We have a free will to do what we want but the loving thing is the Lord protected me that night in that situation and other dangerous situations I found myself in.

My story takes on a different course as I continue to share with you my journey through my timeline. The fight and struggle becomes more so about spiritual warfare. I've had a lot of good times along the way as well but for now I have to talk about the bad with the purpose of showing how the Lord turned my life around. Some things I allowed to happen because I had no backbone to stand up for myself. I had such a deep spirit of low self esteem and self rejection, I didn't know how to assert myself for fear of being rejected. It caused me to find myself in many precarious situations that led to me being abused by men.

I felt lost and confused in a world that often felt cold, mysterious and frightening which caused me to feel bitter and angry. The Lord understood why I was afraid to get close to anyone. Maybe you may have the same fear of getting close to other people. The Lord can heal you of this spirit just as He did me. Though it still may pose its challenges, especially of getting hurt, I trust the Lord will lead me through. I have to remind you again I'm still a work in progress. Many times I've had to fight against the spirits of anger and bitterness.

As you can see I was pretty messed up. I didn't know the Lord was who I was needing and looking for at the time. You see at the time I didn't know this was a dance with Him, I simply had no clue. At the time of my sister's suicide, in 1982, I was studying with Jehovah's Witnesses (JW) and after a year of bible study I got baptized joining the organization. I thought I had come to know the Lord yet I would find out later that I didn't really know Him after many years as a JW. I came away feeling that I had the wrong concept of God as I had been taught by the Watchtower Society (WTS). However, despite the circumstances, my life as a JW was an all good experience along the way. I was able to plant in my heart during those years as a JW many scriptures as I feasted on the Word of God, daily devouring the bible. I studied the bible incessantly as though I were preparing for some huge exam. But at the time it didn't register in my mind that I would be tested in my relationship with the true God as it came to be. I failed many tests due to a lack of knowledge because even though I was consistently studying the Word, I failed to divide the Word of God correctly. This was all due to a lack of understanding and comprehension because of the false doctrines I was taught.

*2 Timothy 2:15 says, "Study to shew thyself approved unto God, a workman that needeth not to be ashamed, **rightly dividing the word of truth**." KJV*

Embrace Truth and Reject Erroneous Doctrines

As I sought truth solely from the bible, the understanding of the outpouring of the Holy Spirit as it is recorded in the book of Acts took on a whole new fresh meaning. *Acts 2: 38-39*

*It says, "Then Peter said unto them, Repent, and be baptized every one of you in the name of Jesus Christ for the remission of sins, and **ye shall receive the gift of the Holy Ghost**. 39 For the promise is unto you, and to your children, and **to all that are afar off, [even] as many as the Lord our God shall call**." KJV*

For the first time I saw and understood the above scripture, *Acts 2:38-39*, like never before. It was as though suddenly the blinders were off and Jesus shined the light on it for me to see and understand. There are gifts that come along with the anointing of the Holy Spirit. The promise of the Holy Spirit was not for a few to be cut off shortly after being poured out as I had been taught. The scripture clearly says it is for "**ALL that are afar off**". We are that generation of the afar off time now, therefore it's for us today. Furthermore, it doesn't say **"some" or "many" that are afar off**. It says, **"ALL"**.....afar off." You, me and everyone else.

*[Acts 1:5 KJV] 5 For John truly baptized with water; but ye shall be **baptized with the Holy Ghost** not many days hence.*

*[Ephesians 1:13-14 KJV] 13 In whom ye also [trusted], after that ye heard **the word of truth, the gospel** of your **salvation**: in whom also after that ye believed , ye were sealed with that **holy Spirit of promise**, 14 Which is the earnest of our inheritance until the redemption of the purchased possession, ..praise of his glory.*

I didn't know that I could be baptized in the Holy Spirit. I didn't understand *Ephesians 1:13-14,* which says the Holy Spirit is a major part of my inheritance. **Halleluyah!** Somehow I passed over those scriptures because I was taught it was only for a certain period of time ending in 1914. JW's taught me that the time was up. Now I know that God is still calling his children into the ARK of safety. He doesn't want any to perish. I know many of their doctrines were rooted in darkness denying the power of God's Holy Spirit for His children. Jesus told the Pharisees, you don't allow the children of God to have the blessings of the kingdom of heaven and they refused to go in or let anyone that followed them to go in. *Matt 23:13*

Deception is everywhere. As I see it, there is something wrong in all the denominations. There can only be **ONE TRUTH, ONE WAY**. Everyone seems to have a piece of truth but not the **WHOLE TRUTH.** We have to get the whole truth for ourselves and ***work out OUR OWN SALVATION*** by studying the bible with the aid of the Holy Spirit. At times, some of us need someone to help us understand the bible. God has anointed some to teach His Word, however, the Holy Spirit is our best teacher in leading us into all truth I believe. Abraham, Moses, David, the twelve disciples, and the apostle Paul can attest to that. *Phil 2:12 John 15:26 John 16:13*

*[John 16:13 NIV] 13 But when he, the Spirit of truth, comes, **he will guide you into all the truth.** He will not speak on his own; he will speak only what he hears.....*

I made it through by the loving care of God. He always has our best interest at heart and therefore we know we can trust him with all of our heart. My story may speak to you if perhaps you have experienced something similar in your life. Possibly you may know someone who suffers with the spirit of rejection. It may be you reading this now. Jesus has led me to write about things that have brought to the surface things I rarely thought about or ever talked about openly.

Don't Feel Sorry For Me

The somewhat surprising upside however has been the cathartic release I have felt during this time. The Lord cleanses us with His cleansing fire, purifying us through and through to sanctify us, setting us apart for His glory. We overcome all tests, trials and tribulation by the blood of the Lamb. Through Jesus we are blameless and perfect in His eyes. The Father sees Jesus' perfect reflection in us. I see the same reflection. The guilt and shame I felt was removed by His Spirit as I sensed His love and compassion for me. It didn't leave overnight, it took some time for me to get to this place. My transparency is for the sole purpose of helping someone else that may be struggling in life with similar issues I struggled with. You can come out of the mud and mire, smelling like a rose. He really changed my life in so many ways. I'm sure you have your story to tell as well.

We each have a testimony in this life that shows we're not perfect but we can follow the lead of the Perfect One. This will always be my testimony forever throughout eternity inside the annals of time. Just think we will each have His story with our story to tell to future generations. It will be our own unique story to tell for the purpose of inspiring others to dance with Jesus forever.

Searching For The Lord

I developed a real genuine relationship with the Lord through the Holy Spirit. It was my experience of the baptism of the Holy Spirit that led me on the journey to get to where I am today. During the early years when I first left the JW organization, I began seeking after God in a whole new way because I was far away from Him. I had gone back to the world and started doing things I had stopped doing as a Christian. Smoking, which is not necessarily a salvation issue, defiles not only our body but our soul and spirit which for me was a hindrance to spiritual growth. I was a backslider, falling into the worst thing I could do, sexual sin. Backslidden, I was lost for several years after leaving the organization until the Lord stepped in. I met someone through online dating who knew and understood the organization I had left but he was also a backslider. He lied about his status, saying he was single but turns out he was a married man. By the time I found out, emotionally invested, it was too difficult to break it off.

There's irony in how God will use someone who's not walking the straight and narrow path to help you get back on it, as He did in my case. In time I got back on the straight and narrow getting baptized again in 2006, only to fall off the wagon backsliding again except only for a moment. My new found faith stirred my interest in an apostolic Pentecostal church. I was baptized in Jesus name according to the scripture in Acts 2:38 which is when I received the baptism of the Holy Spirit.

[Acts 2:38 NIV] *38 Peter replied, "Repent and **be baptized**, every one of you, **in the name of Jesus Christ** for the forgiveness of your sins. And **you will receive the gift of the Holy Spirit.***

For the most part, it's been a close walk and dance with the Lord as I found myself pursuing Him, longing to know Him more intimately. I felt something had been missing in my life. Over time I found the missing link which sparked a steady growth in our relationship. Our dance started out slow as He was teaching me the steps. That hurt little girl had grown up to be a guilt-ridden insecure woman who was feeling unlovable and rejected, disillusioned and confused. It seems I attracted guys that were broken, abusers, drug users, infidels. I remember once going home with a bloody black eye and when my family member asked about it, I was silent. Jesus was the only one I could talk to about anything. Having shut people out, I found a true friend and love in Jesus Christ.

Dining With The Lord

I found **JESUS** to be more real than anything or anyone I ever imagined as our relationship grew. One evening I was having some pains in my stomach. I decided to have a small glass of red wine to relax and calm my stomach. Unexpectedly, the Lord dined with me that night out on the veranda of my townhouse apartment in Plano, Texas. I was feeling lonely, fleeing from fornication, running for my life. *1Cor 6:18* I will never forget this special moment, although I can't tell you what was said during our conversation. *1Tim 5:23 Rev 3:20* Somehow, I just knew Jesus was there with me as I talked to him, feeling His tangible presence. I remember us laughing a lot.

Since then, I think often of how cool it will be to dance in heaven along the river of life reminiscing over this moment, recounting what was said that night. I can't wait to hear what He says was so funny. He's made me laugh a few other times since. His friendship, guardianship and leadership has molded me into a NEW creation in Him, completely transforming me. As our relationship deepened, I came to know HIM in His true nature of LOVE in a personable way. *Proverbs 31:25 Eccles 3:4* He has taught me many things through His Holy Spirit and what I appreciate most is not to take things too seriously.

As such, He led me to create an online ministry website called Hope Devotions which revolves around the fruits of His Spirit which all revolve around LOVE. I came to understand how all the fruits of the Holy Spirit come out of LOVE, love being the parent and all the other fruits are the offspring or siblings of love. I appreciate all He is, His *love, joy, faith, peace, long suffering, temperance, gentleness, meekness and goodness.*

I don't understand people who don't care to have a close relationship with the Lord through His Holy Spirit. Many today are more afraid of the Holy Spirit than of the enemy of God. This fear of the Holy Spirit I'm talking about is not the same as having the fear of the Lord which is a healthy fear, which is a feeling of awe and the desire to not displease God. To truly fear God means to shun evil. Do you have the proper fear of God? Have you thought about it? Some have an **unhealthy fear** of the Holy Spirit actually fearing a close relationship with Him. Shouldn't our biggest fear of all be the fear of being far removed from God. I want to be as close as possible to Him.

It seems the real issue for some is the fear of turning control over to someone else. What they fail to realize is without the Holy Spirit controlling you, your life will be OUT of CONTROL. Being without control of God's Spirit will make one susceptible to the control of God's enemy. This is why many are falling for the lies of the enemy which portray the Holy Spirit as someone or something strange and out of control.

Of course, that's absurd. He's just the opposite, bringing inner peace, stability, self-control and joy of the spirit. I learned through trial and error when we **submit** to God completely and **resist** the devil, the devil will flee. *James 4:7* Submission to God brings gifts of the Spirit which I've been blessed to receive. He's not a respecter of persons, these gifts are for all who ask. One of my gifts is singing in the Spirit, which can lead to beautiful spiritual songs to sing and share. Singing in the Spirit to the Lord is a special treat. To sing to him period is a great source of relaxation.

Colossians 3:16 says, *"Let the message of Christ dwell among you richly as you teach and admonish one another with all wisdom through psalms, hymns, and* **songs from the Spirit**, *singing to God with gratitude in your hearts." NIV*

One of the songs featured on the **"Dance with the King"** CD is called **"Israel, lift up thine eyes"**. The melody and lyrics came as a result of me singing in the Spirit. I embrace the Holy Spirit not only as the giver of gifts but also as the Comforter that he is. As my Savior he has brought me through many trials and tribulations. As my Lord, I saw him in the dream where he said that he wanted to teach me one on one. That is a privilege for every single Christian to have if they want it. I hear the Spirit saying it is for all who will open their hearts and answer the knock at the door of their heart to let Him in. He calls us all to different paths, to walk with Him as He strengthens our personal relationship with Him. I believe He wants that with all of His sheep, not just a select few.

"The Making of Dancing with the King" CD and writing this book has been a labor of love for me as the Lord has led me to co-write and co-labor with Him in this whole project. Our efforts together have produced a **C**hrist **D**irected **CD** that celebrates the wedding of the Bride and Bridegroom. It speaks to the heart of all those anxiously awaiting the arrival of the King of Kings and Lord of Lords. I will share with you the songs I wrote, along with their lyrics following a timeline of sorts to help you understand how the CD was developed over the time it took to create it. It was quite an adventure as you will see.

MY JOURNAL WITH TIMELINE

So far, I wanted to paint a vivid picture laying a clear foundation of who I am and what kind of background I've come from. As I've said before I knew the Lord was always with me through all the trials and fiery tests. Just as the Lord was leading me back then, he is still today leading me in this dance. As we dance together, he continues instructing me of His specific plan and purpose for my life as He does for each one of us.

As you go through the timeline I have put together you will see how the Lord has truly blessed me in spite of the many difficult things I had to go through. I will share with you some of the journal entries from my personal diaries and journals to give you a snapshot of my personal life, including personal bible study notes, dreams, and prophetic words given during one of the most difficult periods of my life.

As a little girl I remember always feeling God was with me. At one point I wanted to become a nun, a cloistered nun at that. By now I think you can understand why I wanted to be a cloistered nun considering the many different orders of nuns there are. Cloistered nuns live a life of solitude for the purpose of intercessory prayer, with quiet meditation and reflection. I felt it would allow me the time and private space to talk to God and draw close to Him. Being a nun was not his plan for me.

My journal timeline begins around the close of the year of 2014. This was a pivotal year in my life's journey on the road to Dancing with the King. One ordinary day became an unforgettable day where I prayed to the Lord to please purify me, to cleanse me because I wanted to be closer to him. It was a simple sincere prayer. What happened after that prayer set me on a road that was dark and ugly and scary as all heck. I had no idea what was on the road up ahead.

This was during a time when speculation was high on social media that the rapture was about to happen. I had been active on social media during 2011-2012 and was busy working on building a ministry website. My interest peaked in 2013 about the coming rapture and I wanted to find other people who were just as excited as I had become about the Lord's return. People in the church didn't seem to have the same intense longing or understanding of the end times. I started researching on the net and of course there's the pre-trib, mid-trib and post-trib theories as well as the preterist view which teaches everything has already been fulfilled. I can't say I understand it.

In this maze of information technology, I joined several rapture watch groups on the internet going back in 2013. Often dates were being thrown about in many forum group websites, or FB and YT, which always failed to come true. After a while you become disheartened after getting your hopes up high. I was caught up in all the drama of the rapture false prophets.

They were giving out false dates and they are still at it. I will talk more on the date setters later on. All Christians should be watching for His return as I am also anxiously awaiting. The Spirit and the bride say, "Come Lord Jesus". Amen On another note, early on in the year of 2014, I went to a seminar for spiritual cleansing through my church. At the time I was still being challenged in walking in complete submission to God. I would learn that deliverance is a gradual process. We have to be fully dedicated to finish the process because it takes time for some. It's not always easy when walking after the Holy Spirit to change our sinful ways.

Isn't it when we are trying to live right our battle against the evil cravings of our fallen flesh intensifies. Six months earlier I'd had the war room dream that ended with Jesus instructing me to follow his lead pointing out warfare strategies.

Here begins my journal timeline...**PRIVATE** entries all for the purpose of helping someone who's reading this book now. It may not always make sense to you. I was a work in progress as I am even so now.

October 2014

10/6/2014 SIGNS OF THE END OF THE AGE

In October of 2014 I was on a quest in my personal bible study about the end times which actually started back in 2006 when I first discovered *Irvin Baxter of End Times Ministry.* He's come a long way since his Indiana days, now he can be seen and heard all over the world including on both major Christian TV stations Daystar and TBN. I studied his tapes, devouring the material after getting hold of an inexhaustible supply line.

I was spiritually starving wanting to understand how the end time prophecies were being fulfilled in our day and time. He actually moved his ministry from Indiana to the church I was a member of in 2006 where I got born again and baptized in Jesus name. On this particular day of 2014 I wrote some interesting conclusions I had come to from my personal bible study. For one I noted in my diary that the time of God's wrath would be a time of **"total mayhem and anarchy-race war"**. I wrote this no doubt referencing the rioting that had been going on in Ferguson, only 20-25 minutes away from where I lived. At one point the rioting did come into my neighborhood. Today as I'm writing this we've been seeing even more incidents like Ferguson come to pass with all the police killings of African Americans, mostly male.

And the African Americans are rioting and protesting as well as killing police officers. What I was looking for at this time was the Lord to guide me in this dark world and to discern his voice amongst all the different voices speaking.

Testing the Spirit

The Lord told me to be careful regarding the messages on YouTube. He told me that not all messages are for you. Some only stir fear in you. These messages are for those that are not repentant, who are holding on to the world. They need to be stirred inside to move them to repentance. The fear of God is what they need.

So you must be choosy about the messages you listen to or read. He told me many of the pictures carried demonic spirits. Full submission to God is obedience. It's listening to the Holy Spirit and obeying His voice. It's not easy. Discipline does not feel good when it's being administered. The Lord was telling me that I needed to take some strong medicine for myself by way of starving my flesh till it dies. He told me that I should fast TV, music, the internet, and rich foods. The carnal flesh is the enemy of God in us. During this time with the Lord, I asked him several questions and he answered me right away. Fast forward a month to November.

November 2014

11/7/2014 PRESENCE OF GOD

"Wow, I was just in the presence of God. I have never felt such joy and the peace that transcends all understanding. He spoke to me about how much he loves me. He told me things about myself that I knew it could only be God. He was pleased with my repentance and even gave me permission to laugh. I told him that I didn't want to hang an art piece I bought which said, LIVE LOVE LAUGH. I said, ``Lord,I wish it said LIVE LOVE LAMENT." I lament not only of my sins but for the sins of our country, our world, the body of Christ.

What he said reminds me of the scripture that says we should confess our sins, repent and in time God will raise us up. He reminded me that He IS in control when we are fully submitted to Him. This is when we can be assured of His powerful presence, and anointing. And it's His anointing that will bring down strongholds in our life. To me God was saying, Faye, I've got this. Stop trying to fight your own battles. Let me fight them for you. I'm not sure what He meant by the next words He said to me. Keep silent, he said. I will do the talking for you. Speak only when I say speak. Follow my direction. "Trust in me with all your heart, lean not on your own understanding. Take notice of me and I will make your paths straight."

As you can see from my journal entry, my mind was in a state of repentance. I had a problem with sexual sin being single. You know what goes along with this kind of sin when in isolation and lonely. In spite of this, the Lord was leading me in my battle through his warfare strategy. He gave me another word a few days later that was not just for me.

11/11/2014 TIME FOR ALL TO REPENT

Those who love the world will be left in the world. I am coming soon to take you home. I will wipe away all tears from your eyes. There will only be tears of joy. Repent of your sins. Leave your evil ways. Love like never before. Remove the bitterness from your heart. You do this by asking me to remove it. The Holy Spirit will guide you in all things. He is your friend.

He will lead you to green pastures to lie down in peace. Tranquility will greet you with a smile. Cherish your time on the earth now. It is a special time to be alive on earth. It is a time to live for the King of Kings and Lord of Lords. He will remember you when you come to live in the kingdom. He will share his kingdom with you. Now is the time to repent. Wail and cry before the throne of grace. Now is the time of judgment for the church. Your God is revealing hearts, cleansing hearts, purifying hearts that are bent in spirit. Prostrate yourself before the Lord. Many have bitterness in their hearts towards me and their brother. There should be no bitter root in you. Some are bitter because the rapture is delayed in their mind because they had a SET date in mind. Setting specific dates is not good for you. But keep looking up, keep watching for my return." This is a powerful word that speaks to the times we are living in. Each day we come a day closer to his return. We must look for him everyday because He will come as a thief to those who are not looking. Many are tired after being disillusioned with the false prophets of date setting. So some have given up and stopped looking. Their oil lamps are running out of oil. We must keep our oil lamps full. A week later Nov 18th; after I received this word, I began a fast and continued proceeding down the road of repentance. It was the beginning of a long battle of spiritual warfare on the road of cleansing and deliverance. The second day I broke the fast so I started again on Thursday.

11/20/2014 THURSDAY - Day 2

This is not easy to recount this time in my life. I continued the fast, day 2 bringing on one of the most horrific experiences I've ever experienced. This was during the time of the Michael Brown riots here in St. Louis. It was on a cold damp night that the enemy was attacking me and I was praying for the Lord to deliver me. I couldn't stay in my apartment. It was around midnight that I got in my car half dazed, praying in tongues. I was driving with my windows down freezing, spirits coming out barking like dogs, laughing, taunting me.

I was balling my eyes out crying out to God. I finally made it back home after only God knows how long I was out driving like a mad woman.

11/21/2014 FRIDAY - Day 3

This was quite an eventful day. I began the day by talking to a stranger I found on the internet who tried to help me by praying for me but she couldn't help me. Partly I was afraid, the spirit of fear had set in. My sexual sins had opened me up to these demonic spirits of lust and God knows what else. Also I dabbled in the occult in high school. You know how it is when you get a ouija board for Christmas or sit around with your family at home or classmates at a school retreat telling ghost stories. It was all coming back to haunt me though I had long ago repented of all of this.

I thought to myself, I can go to my church, the church I belonged to and get the Pastor to lay hands on me. There were no pastors in the church office when I got there I was told. Just as I was leaving, in came a Pastor that I knew and felt comfortable with. I could see that was the Lord's doing. He told me how he prayed to keep his family covered and laid hands on me and prayed for me. I could discern the discomfort after I told him what was happening with me, that demons were touching me in my private area. That's not something you want to tell anybody let alone a man.

But I was humbled by this whole situation and embarrassed. The only way I can talk about it now is in the hopes that someone else who may be going through this will know they are not alone or crazy. I had my day somewhat planned out so I had packed a lunch to have a picnic with the Lord at the park. I took along elements for communion. It was a sunny day so after leaving the church I went and parked my car at the park.

I communed and talked with the Lord, read some scriptures and then took communion. I called a girlfriend who lives out of town to fill her in on what was going on. She encouraged me and prayed for me. As I was on my way home I spoke to another friend who went to my church and she told me my problem could be cured if I would take a bath in salt and put salt all around me. I know it sounds crazy but desperate people do desperate things.

Filling my tub with salt, I soaked in it as I prayed for I don't know how long. But guess what? Did that end the problem? No, of course not. I found out later in my research this is really a superstition. Practicing a superstition is displeasing to God. So I was opening more doors to the enemy which made me vulnerable to more attacks. I reached out to a pastor for help in a church I had visited from time to time after speaking with my girlfriend who lived in another state again. I knew she was a prayer warrior. She encouraged me again, praying for me.

I called the pastor and when I told him my problem he put me on the phone with his wife. Bottom line they didn't believe Christians could be possessed by demons so they didn't really understand or comprehend the situation I was in.

Later that night after midnight I was again engaged in spiritual warfare. I was again in my car, windows rolled down, freezing cold. Just like the night before many were coming out screaming, barking etc. Feeling desperate I called the same pastor again because I had his cell phone number in my contacts list on my cell phone. He basically told me to call him back in the morning or come by the church during the time of their Saturday morning bible study. After more fighting and deliverance, I made my way back home.

11/22/2014 SATURDAY - Day 4

Saturday was a beautiful sunny day with blue skies and white clouds. It was warming up a bit outside and I was ready to get on with the business at hand. I was praying to the Lord for help and seeking him the best I could. I got in my car and drove to the church instead of calling. No one was there so I called him. I believe I must have gotten the time wrong but he said, Faye come to church tomorrow and we'll all get around you and pray for you. The thing was I needed help right then. I drove around for hours and finally went back home. I called the lady I had found on the internet again and she said okay we are going to pray and get you all cleaned out. So I left my apartment driving in my car because I didn't want to release these spirits inside my home. Now I know how to pray for myself but at this time I needed someone to help me. She started praying for me after I parked my car in the parking lot.

For some reason nothing was working and she started getting frustrated with me telling me I didn't want to cooperate with her. She said to me, honey I can't help you. Just keep praying and they will all come out. I started driving in my car off of the lot and kept praying to the Lord, crying out to Jesus. And they started coming out again barking and screaming so much so I almost couldn't get pulled over quick enough. I pulled over to another lot and started puking and coughing. My hair was a mess, I looked like a wild woman. I was so distraught as I crawled out of my car. Now standing, I saw a woman walking a dog but I could barely stand. I asked her if she could help me.

She looked startled and fearful of me. I could hear her thoughts it seemed. I imagined her saying, "lady , you are crazy." At this point, I agreed with what I imagined she was saying. Feeling desperate and embarrassed, I asked, mam, is there a church around here where I can go that specializes in deliverance? She tried to give me directions to a nearby church but I couldn't find the church. So I headed back home feeling worse than ever and more desperate for help. I managed to make it through the night.

11/23/2014 SUNDAY - Day 5

I was on my way to my church but I couldn't make it. I got off the highway and just drove around in circles. I was beaten down, weak from the fasting and just in really bad shape. My heart was aching and crying out for deliverance. I had so many bondages in my life. Finally I realized I wasn't going to make it to church but our church had another campus in the city close to where I was at. I knew service was by now ending but I just wanted to talk to the Pastor and get him to help me. Just as I drove up the young pastor was standing on the sidewalk helping someone get on the van. It was just starting to rain and he looked over at me at the moment I jumped out of my car. He walked over to me standing by the car covering us both with his umbrella. He had such a compassionate look of concern on his face as I cried to him, telling him about my problem. I could see in his face the deep sadness he was feeling for me as I described the emotional and mental anguish I was in.

He laid his hand on me and prayed for me. I went home feeling better but I knew the battle was not over. It's still not over as I'm writing this book right now. In spite of it all, I leave everything in the Lord's hand. I take refuge in Him alone. I serve and worship Him alone. I fear Him alone. I stand on His Word and have faith in all of his promises knowing that the enemy is defeated. We overcome by the blood of the lamb and our testimony.

Our testimonies are not fully written yet but someday they will be, to serve as an eternal blessing to others. Let's make sure our testimony will end with our remaining faithful and loyal to the Lord. As I'm writing this I am balling my eyes out as I recall the pain and anguish I felt in my soul. The song, **"Walking with Jesus Along the River of Life"** , an instrumental, is on repeat in my ITunes playlist.

I thank the Holy Spirit for giving me this precious gift of a song. It is a rendition of **"La Boda"** where I'm playing the flute voice on my keyboard. It transports me in a place of peace and tranquility knowing how much my Lord loves me. He was with me everyday throughout this whole process of spiritual cleansing and spiritual warfare. I was willing to go to any and all lengths because I love Him that much to get cleansed. I want to be pure and holy in my walk with Him. I'm not perfect and I still fall short of perfection but my heart is perfectly aligned with His in my love for righteousness and his laws and commandments.

One last note is that I want to make something perfectly clear and that is that I appreciate all of the pastors I reached out to, to help me. Unfortunately out of the four only one was equipped to really help me. The other three wanted to help but they couldn't handle me. I could tell they were not used to people like me. I got the feeling they had never really dealt with deliverance or issues of my gravity.

Shortly after that, my Pastor did a special conference on deliverance, sort of like self deliverance tools. It was somewhat helpful and I learned some things especially about how it doesn't always happen overnight. Bottom line everyone did the best they could as far as trying to help me. Some things have to be walked out with the Lord and Him alone. Though I'm still learning. I may have said this but we have to work out our own salvation with fear and trembling.

[Phil 2:12 KJV] *12 Wherefore, my beloved, as ye have always obeyed, not as in my presence only, but now much more in my absence,* **work out your own salvation** *with fear and trembling.*

Added commentary: 5/19/2021 Many are walking around in bondage today, some knowingly and some not knowing. In both cases, as long as you don't rock the boat and confront the enemy, evicting him, they will remain quiet because they have you under their control. It's when you give the enemy an eviction notice the warfare begins.

I've learned to take authority over the enemy as the Lord has given to us as his disciples **Luke 10:19** ...also I learned to call upon the Lord to fight for me taking refuge in Him. He will fight for me just as sure as He fought for Moses and Joshua in their battles. Glory to God! Today I am delivered and free. These journal entries will help you appreciate what I went through to get my deliverance. Though today I'm delivered, it's a fight that continues daily to crucify the flesh. We must fight our flesh til the day we die.

December 2014

12/13/2014 TRUTH MATTERS

During my personal bible study I made note of two scriptures I wanted to commit to memory. 1 John 1:8-9 and 2 Corinthians 1:20-21. John speaks about how we can deceive ourselves if we say we have no sin which means the truth is not in us. If we confess our sins, he is faithful to forgive us.

*[2 Corinthians 1:20-22 NIV] 20 For **no matter how many promises God has made**, they are **"Yes" in Christ**. And so through him the "Amen" is spoken by us to the glory of God.*

21 Now it is God who makes both us and you stand firm in Christ. He anointed us, 22 set his seal of ownership on us, and put his Spirit in our hearts as a deposit, guaranteeing what is to come.

My personal notes on these two scriptures I want to share with you because it speaks of my mind frame at the time. My writing is not always coherent due to the frame of mind I was in and I'm still dealing with the spiritual cleansing and warfare. Part of the strategy of the enemy is to keep telling you your sins are not forgiven. The purpose is to keep us in condemnation and feeling guilty even though we've confessed our sin and fully repented and have been fully forgiven.

Personal notes:

Truth is what I want to take a hold of and grab and never let it go. That's what is worth everything I have to give or give up to obtain it and keep it. Truth matters. It sets us free from the deceptive lies of the enemy.

The truth is we are sons and daughters of the Most High God, the God of Abraham, Isaac and Jacob, Father Yahweh (Jehovah) and Yeshua (Jesus). His blood has cleansed us of ALL our sins (not just some). Therefore, we are no longer separated from God but are drawn near. We can even come boldly before the throne of grace to ask what we need and we can expect to receive. I wrote out the following scriptures in my bible study notebook. This was a day of meditating on many scriptures including these about maintaining and walking in holiness. *1Pet 1: 14-16, 2 Cor 7:1, 1Pet 2:9, 1John 3: 6-10, 1Thess 4:7, Heb 12:14, Lev 20:26 and Phil 4:8*

12/25/14 WORDS OF LOVE @ 2AM

Lord I love you so much
I want to be with you always
This is my love song to sing to you
For eternity, forever into the third day
I saw a vision of you and I
Dancing under a clear blue sky
You took me by the hand, twirled me around
We laughed as our feet left the ground

Sounds like the good beginning of a great song one day. I just discovered these words as I was writing this book. I'm not sure if they were my words but I believe so because they were hand written on scrap paper with the time written on it. It speaks to what's in my heart...dancing with the King of Kings.

January 2015

1/7/2015 A NEW BEGINNING

Thank you Lord for a New Year and New Beginnings. By now you have read and come to know the last few months of 2014 were quite challenging for me indeed. Therefore, I wanted to start the New Year with a clear focus on the Lord having made some new spiritual goals for myself. As the Lord led me, my overall plan targeted not only my spiritual health but physical and emotional as well. I chose to do this by fasting with lots of prayer and bible reading. I began following a 10 day Daniel fast starting on January 7, 2015. During the fast I kept a daily video journal and a written journal to follow my progress, taking notes to highlight any special revelations or lessons learned. Here's one journal entry I found interesting that was made the day after finishing my 10 day Daniel fast:

*"I was in a **hot pursuit of the Lord**, truly spiritually blessed during my fast. I learned a healthier way of eating, cooking food cooked with kosher salt, like beans and rice, and mixed vegetables. Food that is pure and healthy in its natural state, without preservatives or additives. I **fasted YouTube and all social media** to consume **God's Word without additives or fillers**."*

Drawing close to God was my number one priority above anything. It meant everything to me to hear his voice above the enemy's voice including my own voice. I learned that the enemy's voice at times, most times is easy to detect because it is cruel, mean, evil and vulgar. Our own voice as well can be deceiving, telling us what we want to hear. God's voice is always in harmony with his written Word, for he is the same yesterday, today and forever.

[Hebrews 13:8] *"Jesus Christ the same yesterday, and today, and forever."* **KJV**

During this time of fasting I wrote out a five page prayer that was an inside view of all the issues and desires of my heart.

I can see where some things have been answered but many have not. God's timing is something we must respect and wait on. Learning to trust him is implicit but it doesn't happen overnight. Nevertheless, during times when we may feel stressed, spiritually, emotionally and mentally strained is when God in his strength works on our behalf. He promises to never leave us nor forsake us. He will not put on us more than we can bear but will make a way out if necessary.

[1Cor 10:13] *"No temptation has overtaken you except what is common to mankind. And God is faithful; he will not let you be tempted beyond what you can bear. But when you are tempted, he will also provide a way out so that you can endure it."* **NIV**

I came to appreciate pure healthy food, lots of fresh vegetables and fruit with whole grains. More importantly, I gained a new perspective towards my life in a positive way.

I acquired a taste for healthy spiritual food, the pure unadulterated word of God. This was all part of the ongoing one on one training with the Lord that I had dreamt about back in 2013. He is the greatest teacher ever, still training me. He was then and always will be my refuge. I would learn to lean on him even more in the days, weeks and months ahead.

1/8/2015 APOLOGY NOT ACCEPTED

2014 was the time when serious spiritual cleansing began in my life. I was doing a lot of praying and fasting. As mentioned earlier, I came under severe spiritual attack by the enemy and I didn't know how to fight this spiritual battle. I didn't understand how to use our spiritual weapons of warfare nor did I have the knowledge or know how to just let go and let God fight my battles. This was one of the most difficult periods of my life. Much of the time we can quote the right scriptures and know what the prescription calls for when we know what ails us but until we apply the scriptures fully and take the medicine God prescribes for us we will remain spiritually sick.

Here I am on day two of my ten day fast. At this point in my life though I was making a few strides in my efforts of spiritual warfare against the enemy with the Lord's help and strategy, however; the enemy will never cut us any slack.

If he can't come at you one way, he will come in another way. For example, a dear minister had provided covering for my first online ministry website.

I had worked hard for two years to build it. I will not mention the name of the ministry website nor go into any details of what happened but we had a falling out, a misunderstanding and parted our ways. I was truly devastated at the time and really hurt over the situation in what had transpired. At the same time I was confused by the enemy and didn't even know it at the time. The best I could do was send a note of sincere apology after our last less than pleasant phone conversation. I never got a response back from the minister, my brother in the Lord concerning my email apology, so in my mind the apology was never accepted.

Several months later I sent another email trying to make peace and amend the situation. I read that email a few days ago as I'm writing this book in 2016 and saw that what I wrote and the scripture I sent made no sense. Actually it made matters worse in my opinion because of how the scripture could and probably was misconstrued. Without going into details I dug myself into a deeper hole with this person I believe. What I learned in all of this is when we do things out of our flesh, reacting and speaking out of our emotions, it plays right into the hands of the enemy. Even though I was trying to reach out and make things better, it would have been wise on my part to consult the Lord about the situation first and thereby leave it in his hands. So now finally I have done that, leaving the situation in the Lord's hand.

He knows what is truly in my heart, knowing our fight is not really against flesh and blood but against wicked spirits in high places. I can see how the enemy brought the spirit of confusion in my life but again what can you do? You can't go back and erase what has been written, said or done. And because the person refuses to talk with me gives the enemy more ground in the situation. But that is ONLY if I let him. The Lord taught me in all this drama, much of which I brought on myself to not be overly concerned about how others see you, feel about you, judge your heart motives, etc. We're all tested in different ways. I have learned in everything now to let go and let God in situations that I have no control over.

I can't control what someone thinks about me. In this case things got to the point that whatever I would say or try to do to make things better made things worse. As I look back at some of these things I've gone through, only with God being there could I have made it through. I'm the type of person that hates drama or having someone upset with me. I want everyone to like me. Are you saying, me too? If not, I say good for you. Through this personality conflict and situation I didn't give up on myself, moreover, I didn't give up on God. And best of all, God did not give up on me. He continued working with me, teaching me about myself through others and other means.

He was leading me to this very project **CD** and book, **"Dancing with the King of Kings"**.

I had no idea where he was leading me at the time. I simply had to trust and follow his direction and not allow this situation or any situation to detract me from where he was leading me. I suppose my brother in the Lord was doing the same thing, not allowing my hang ups or issues to detract him from his God given assignment. God will never give up on any of us because we are all his children. He loves us ALL so much.

1/19/2015 WORD FROM THE LORD

My ten day Daniel fast ended on Friday, January 16, 2015. Even though the fast started out with my having an unfortunate misunderstanding and conflict with my dear brother in the Lord somehow I stayed on track and stuck with the fast for all ten days without cheating. I remember Sunday, the 18th, just two days after the fast, I was preparing to go visit a friend's church. I had already gone to my own church service that morning and my friend's church service didn't start until 3:30pm. As I was preparing myself to go, the Lord started speaking to my spirit. He gave me an encouraging Word for their church and I shared it with the congregation during service. I hadn't seen them for a while because their church is quite a distance from where I live. I deeply love my friends who are a beautiful married couple.

They are both pastors that moved from California to start a church in a suburb of St. Louis.

Later that night as I was falling off to sleep on the couch, the Lord nudged me to sit up and start writing a specific Word to give them. I could hear God's voice again just as I had earlier that day. His voice was clear and precise, not audible but in my spirit, the still small voice. I wrote everything down that the Lord said and emailed my friends the word right away around 1:30 am. They each sent me individual emails expressing gratitude and confirmed that it was a message from the throne room of heaven, directly from God.

The word addressed specific things that only they and the Lord would know. God does answer prayers. He not only answered my prayer to hear his voice clearly as I had prayed during the fast but answered their prayers through the word he gave me for them. I was so blessed that God would use me in this way to bless my friends with a word directly from Him and earlier a word for their congregation. To God be ALL the Glory!!! Praise God!!!

February 2015

2/1/2015 FREEDOM TO CHOOSE

God made us all free moral agents giving us the freedom to choose between right and wrong. His ways are perfect and upright, good for our body, spirit and soul.

On Sunday, February 1, 2015 I made a profound statement, cleansing my heart before God which was part of my training and discipline from the Lord. The transparency you see in my writing is not as easy as you may think perhaps while you are reading this book. Sometimes I say to God, really Lord I don't want to share this. Then, he says, *"Yes, you do because it will help someone else that's struggling with the same struggles you have. You will give them hope in knowing I am a God that pardons the most grievous of sin. I delight in those with a contrite heart and spirit. When you humble yourself before me, I will raise you up. Your testimony is a testament to that."* Convinced it is God's will, I gave Him my word that I would be honest, truthful and fully transparent. But God only with your help can I do this.

JOURNAL ENTRY: 2/1/2015

Each one of us has the freedom to choose as to what we will do. I choose to crucify my flesh and walk after God. I choose you God, God of Abraham, Isaac and Jacob.

You I choose, your will over my own. I may even have the desire to please myself but I deny my flesh of those debased desires that I used to give in to. Why, why do I deny my flesh now when I used to give in to it. For one, I had convinced myself that I could always ask God to forgive me, I could always say oh, it's a weakness.

I could always say, well self gratification, masturbation it's not really wrong because it's nowhere in the bible. So I had reasoned with myself to do this detestable act, saying it was okay. But in reality, it was not okay and deep down in my soul I knew it was wrong. But it was something of a habit, a bad habit learned over many years. But I finally came to the realization how displeasing this act is to the Lord and wanted to come clean before the Lord, asking the Lord to cleanse me with his fire, asking him to purify me. Asking for his baptism of fire. I wrote a poem to the Lord asking to be made whole again. I was broken in spirit. On the altar of repentance I danced before the Lord boldly as Jesus led me there, to the cross to crucify my flesh.

Poem to the Lord:

Jehovah Jehovah Jehovah
I boldly come before your throne
I ask to be made whole
A complete heart is what I have to give
I'll crucify my flesh that again I may live

March 2015

3/3/15 RENEWED STRENGTH

THIS WAS A TIMELY MUCH NEEDED WORD FROM THE LORD.

I will give you renewed strength. Be encouraged. Some things will seem to remain as they are because you have taken a stand against them. Now lay them at the altar of repentance, there I will wipe away your tears and restore your joy before me".

[James 4:7-10 NIV] 7 **Submit yourselves,** then, to God. **Resist** the devil, and he will **FLEE** from you. 8 Come near to God and he will come near to you. Wash your hands, you sinners, and purify your hearts, you double-minded. 9 Grieve, mourn and wail. Change your laughter to mourning and your joy to gloom. 10 **Humble** yourselves before the Lord, and he will **LIFT** you up.

When you fall, get back up. I had apparently fallen again into sin. This word proved to be even more so a prophetic word that let me know though the battle was still waging, it would seem to be a losing battle at times in the coming months. All because I had taken a stand for righteousness, my battle would rage on against the enemy in my flesh. I had not learned yet to RESIST the sin and temptations that would come at me as I should.

There was head knowledge but learning to fully apply the principles of James 4:7-10 would take some time. Yet God was holding my hand assuring me of his unlimited grace and mercy through a Father's steady hand of discipline. As I meditated on his word spoken to my spirit as well as his written Word, I was supernaturally strengthened as He said I would be.

JOURNAL ENTRY 3/31/15:

DNA Divine **N**ature of the **A**lmighty (**A**bba)

As I'm writing this today on January 8, 2017 at 2:40pm I'm reminded of the secret place we have in the Lord. The battle would continue to wage but I was sticking close to the Lord. We were dancing a beautiful waltz to music that I would later hear in my spirit and record. One of the benefits of keeping a journal is being able to go back to a specific point in time and see where you were in your walk and dance with the Lord. In my case on March 31, 2015 it was a good place in spite of what I had thus far gone through.

JOURNAL ENTRY 3/31/15:

Words in ( ) added for clarification:

*"Quiet time this morning with the Lord. He spoke to my spirit that I now have a new **DNA**. I have His **DNA** - the **D**ivine **N**ature of the **A**lmighty, the **D**ivine **N**ature of **A**bba. I began this conversation with the Lord just meditating and thinking*

upon the things of my home, heaven. (In the conversation), I started describing myself as I saw myself in heaven laying down in a beautiful meadowland, a field of green grass and colorful flowers. Jesus is there (listening to me) *and there are also a couple of angels. There are all kinds of little critters playing around us. I see grapes, wine, cheese, matzo crackers, chocolates and more. The birds are singing praises to God Almighty and I am singing along with all the critters around us to the King of Kings and Lord of Lords in our midst. I lay back laughing deep belly laughs as the angels tell us stories of their experiences on earth. Jesus smiles the entire time listening earnestly. He tells me in my spirit as I think upon this moment in heaven with him that I am not to forget I can come up anytime I want because I am seated in heavenly places with him. I abide in him now. This is my inheritance.*

(It is also your inheritance if you belong to Christ.) *Also I felt in my spirit that this is the secret place, it's a place in heaven, any place in heaven, it's a place in our spirit, in our heart with God's heart. I'm describing a place in my heart of imagination as I imagined it would be in heaven. I'm not saying I literally went to heaven. You can have that place, your heart in God's heart revealed to you when you seek him with ALL your heart. Only those who have gone there in faith will understand the full meaning of these words". This place was in my heart and by* **FAITH** *I went there imagining what heaven will be like to me.*

To you heaven may be a day sitting on a bench with Jesus eating ice cream watching people walk along the river of life enjoying their day. Whatever heaven means to you, go there through meditation as it tells us in Colossians to think upon the things of heaven.

[Colossians 3:1-2 NIV] 1 Since, then, you have been raised with Christ, set your hearts on things above, where Christ is, seated at the right hand of God. 2 Set your **MINDS** on **THINGS ABOVE,** not on earthly things.

April 2015

4/2/2015 MORNING MANNA WITH LOVE

Now I'm learning to follow the Lord's lead in our dance. Though at the time I was not hearing the sound of COMPLETE victory quite yet. I was dancing with each step to the sound and melodies of FAITH, LOVE, HOPE and TRUST. God now spoke to my heart to start an online ministry blog called **"Morning Manna with Love" (MMWL)**. The purpose of **MMWL** is to share the love of God the Father **YaHWeH** and Jesus our Lord, Saviour and King. Jesus being the reflection of the Father is the very essence of LOVE. He is the true MANNA, the bread that came down from heaven. God wanted me to begin sharing some of the expressions of His love given to me through inspirational words consisting of bible study articles, poems and songs that are accentuated by the scriptures. As his Holy Spirit leads me, simplicity is my motto. There's nothing fancy about **MMWL**. Jesus told me one day to always try to keep things simple.

Over time the blog has developed into a wonderful website that has blessed many of my Facebook and email group of friends. Have a look.

http://www.morningmannawithlove.weebly.com In the first few months it kept me really busy. I devoted time for personal bible study, meditation and of course writing and rewriting.

It can be very time consuming but it has been all worth the effort. I give God ALL the GLORY. It was on the blog that I began to introduce my friends to some of the songs and music the Lord was inspiring me to write. **Added 10/25/2023 Best of all, it's been a great vehicle to share the gospel as well, to teach the word and encourage my brothers and sisters in the Lord. Nothing is more important than saving souls.** Many times I've shared word messages the Lord has given me. Unfortunately, a few times the spirit of deception, even self deception and confusion creeped in to rob me of the gains and strides I was making thus far in the Lord. It can be humbling to admit a word put forth as thus saith the Lord is not thus saith the Lord.

I always pray now about a word before I release it. The enemy knew I was a babe as far as hearing the voice of the Lord. My priority in all things is to do the will of God and to be pleasing to Him. I have to rebuke the spirits of pride which is an open door to lying, seducing spirits and the spirit of confusion. God is not the author of confusion. I learned over the years that God will never contradict His written Word in any Word He gives. This is the true litmus test more so than anything in my opinion.

I say that because someone else can confirm a word we speak, saying the same thing. But really what does that prove in and of itself alone. The enemy can speak the same exact words of deception to someone else that he spoke to me or you. I thank the Holy Spirit for revealing this to me. I remember when I began the blog, I named it Morning Manna with Faith, Faith being me. Then I felt in my heart a conviction stemming from my selfish pride. I repented before the Lord, changing the name to Morning Manna with Love. You see, Morning Manna with Faith would have been just as appropriate had it not been about me. Most would assume Faith was referring to the principle of faith. Yet that was not the case. How dare I imply in a subtle way that morning manna would be coming from me. LOVE turned out to be the perfect word to represent the ministry the Lord was putting in my hand because it is ALL ABOUT THE LORD. I felt strongholds of pride literally lift off of me that day when I repented before the Lord in prayer after I had changed the name. Glory to God!!! He gets all the glory, honor and praise.

4/12/2015 BRIDAL CHAMBER

The Lord's word gave me lots of comfort when he gave me a personal word of encouragement. He spoke to my inner soul, my heart which I really needed at this time. *"He loves you and wants you to succeed. He is pleased with you. You are now clinging to him as you trust in him. He made you from the dust."* God wants us to be happy. It's the enemy who comes along to discourage us, the enemy comes to kill, steal and destroy our hopes and dreams but Jesus came to give us LIFE.

[John 10:10-11 NIV] 10 *The thief comes only to steal and kill and destroy; I have come that they may have life, and have it to the full. 11 "I am the good shepherd. The good shepherd lays down his life for the sheep.*

For some reason I asked the Lord, why are things so different now? He said to me you are in the bridal chamber. He explained that before now, I could hear him give me words of exhortation and teachings, but (Gifts do come without repentance not that I was not repenting). He further said, *"You never really tried to get to know the person behind the words of inspiration"*. Why? Because there was a reason for sure. I had things and habits that had hindered me from reaching out to get closer to the Lord as I so desperately wanted to. Things like TV and the internet were big distractions among other things. Another big hindrance was that big ugly spirit of pride. What I heard in my spirit astounded me in a good way.

"Now you are the wonderful woman you've always wanted to be. The Lord's been giving you beauty treatments all the while. He has been transforming you from the inside."

Even in our imperfect state, if our heart is aligned correctly in wanting to do what is right, He sees past our imperfections. I was being blessed by the Lord for submitting to the purification PROCESS. At times, in spite of my weaknesses and my insecurities, the Lord used a firm hand of discipline on me. He led me in dance steps I was unprepared for nor liked. It's difficult to describe. What I'm trying to say is this was a dance of complicated movements.

At times it was discouraging when I would take my eyes off of the Lord and take notice of the enemy taunting me with temptation, with suggestions that God was not pleased with me and would not use me.

He would suggest no one would ever listen to me because of my mistaken words attributed to the Lord. Not being fully secure in who I was in Christ at the time made me overly concerned about what others thought of me. Yet God was disciplining me by convicting my conscience and purifying me, He gave me new gifts and added responsibilities of a new ministry blog. Spending time in the chamber was a time of intimacy where I received revelations of his unconditional LOVE. The Lord is coming for a PURE bride. It was a dance that transcended me into a spirit place that showcased His GRACE and MERCY towards me. As I reminisce in the spirit I can understand why GRACE is the meaning of my middle name. Here I was a sinner that at times in the past was addicted to pornography which defiled my spirit with some things I can't even talk about.

However, the BLOOD is powerful enough to cleanse and purify what was once filthy, dirty and disgusting. At times I would feel cleansed and at other times not so much because I had not learned to keep focused on Jesus yet nor fully appreciate how powerful the BLOOD of Jesus really is. I knew enough to appreciate what had been given to me through the chamber of consecration.

It's here we're being beautified through the Holy Spirit. The more I focused on the revelation spoken to my spirit that I was in the chamber, the more I followed His dance steps.

4/15/2015 PERMISSION GRANTED

A word came from the Lord on this Wednesday morning to encourage my soul. This was a powerful word that I journaled from the Lord, a time specially ordained of God. For He orders our steps. This word helped me to understand how many who walk in the gift of the prophetic have their own distinct voice in speaking the words of the Lord. He stores the words in our heart and we take the words and express them in ways that only we can do. And it's all with his permission. You will understand when you read the amazing word Jesus gave me.

"Although the enemy now lies in wait he's under your feet. For now it's too late, my BLOOD covers you at the Cross of affliction. My GRACE covers you at the altar of repentance. I am Jesus the Word of God and I give you many words to use. My words are pliable in your hands to glorify God. You are permitted to take the words I give you to create messages from the depth of my heart. Many words have been stored in you my child." John 3:34, Psalm 119:11, Jeremiah 20:9

4/19/2015 DELIVERANCE OF LUST SPIRITS

As I mentioned before I came to learn that total deliverance does not always happen all at once. The Lord had helped me to appreciate that I was in the chamber like Queen Esther in the book of Esther, having beauty treatments to transform me on the inside. However, that doesn't change the fact that I am still being attacked by these lust spirits. I had inadvertently opened doors to them because of my past behavior of self gratification but more so because of watching pornography on the internet. Some may be surprised that women are just as challenged as men in these areas of life because of our fallen sinful flesh.

JOURNAL ENTRY 4/19/2015:

Yesterday (4/18/2015) I prayed to the Lord asking him where he wanted me to go to church. I had been visiting different churches that were close to my home. The church I belonged to was far from where I lived. Sunday morning I was thinking of going to a neighborhood church because going to my church would mean me being late. But the Lord spoke to my spirit saying I should go to my church. I followed his direction and went even though I was at least twenty minutes late. Determined to get my deliverance from what is now oppressing spirits, after church service I approached the pastor. I told him about the spirits touching me and another minister (a brother) walked up as I was telling the pastor my problem. He turned right to the brother and said to him, Oh she has been having a problem with spirits of lust and they are touching her.

I wanted to crawl underneath something, anything at that moment would have worked. Why would he share something so intimate without my permission just like that yet now I'm sharing it with you. Did he not know what it took for me to even open up and share something so private with him at that moment. I sucked it all in looking away as he said we are going to pray for you now. They both laid hands on me and immediately I fell down on the floor. The Lord was cleansing me. I felt them leaving me (spirits) but I felt so vulnerable and so ashamed lying there on the floor alone. I had never felt so alone as I did that moment on the floor. Yet now I know in my heart that my Lord Jesus was there on the floor with me.

I finally got up knowing people were still inside the sanctuary standing around nearby looking. The pastor and the brother were standing there waiting for me to get up. I know the Pastor was doing what he had to do and knew he had to share my problem for them to minister effectively. But at the time it felt awful. **Just a side note here:** I really didn't have to go through all of this embarrassment.

I didn't have to go through the battles of experiencing them leaving, at times barking and making all kinds of different noises. No I could do like many people do, and that is nothing. Just live with them. They won't bother you if you don't bother them. If we just live in our flesh and do whatever pleases our flesh, we can live pretty comfortably by comparison. So many give up the fight and give in when the road gets tough.

The narrow road we have to walk is worth it in the end. The Lord will see us through to the end. It will take me a while to get the victory but I did get it in time. Now back to my journal.

JOURNAL ENTRY 4/20/2015: *journal with prayer*

This is a personal journal entry which consists mainly of a heartfelt repentance prayer and pleas to the Lord about my use of one seven letter word. I felt my use of this particular word was used in the wrong way and I was feeling guilty about it. The enemy was attacking my mind and I was really in a weak spiritual state of mind. I was dealing with guilt feelings that surrounded two poems I had written in 2013 called Love Tapestry 1 & 2. These poems were profound in meaning to me more than anything at the time it seemed. The poems were based on expressions of God's love for his bride church and all creation as well as our love in return for him the bridegroom. The poems were inspired by the meanings of a number of group member names. These two poems were truly anointed I believe from God, however somehow they had gotten tainted with some expressions I questioned to be seducing spirits of lust. Everywhere I looked at this point in time had the fingerprints of the seducing spirits of lust. Although my heart and motives were pure, I was insecure in my walk with God because of my current condition of mind.

I was in a fierce battle wanting to be cleansed and purified, delivered of any and all aspects of these spirits of lust.

At this time some in the church were taking the fact that we are the bride of Christ way too far as far as I was concerned. Many made it more about a carnal romance than a spiritual romance and it continues that way today. Therefore I started questioning the meanings of words I used in one of my songs I had written and some of the expressions used in my poems of the Love Tapestry. I began to second guess everything I did, said, or wrote. Now as I look back I can see how effective the enemy was in keeping me deceived thinking I was guilty of something I had been forgiven for by the blood of Jesus. The blood cleanses us of ALL of our sins, past, present and future. What we must do is walk after the spirit trusting in Jesus to lead us in his righteousness and holiness and not our own righteousness. We will forever fall short on our own because our flesh will never be perfect and it is impossible to be perfect in our own strength. But with God all things are possible. We can walk closely with Him on the narrow road and allow GRACE to do what we cannot do. We cannot be justified in our own works. Grace justifies us through faith in Christ. Glory to God. But if only I would have understood all this back then, it would have saved me a lot of heartache and pain. I'm so thankful that God set me free of this erroneous belief that led to overwhelming guilt and self-condemnation. But there is no condemnation for those who are in Christ Jesus. However, my testimony will help someone who is challenged in the same test to understand what they must do to get the victory.

The victory is in Christ. The prayer was long but here is an excerpt of the prayer I wrote down that morning.

Excerpt of prayer:

"Heavenly Father, I come before (your) throne, throne of grace and mercy. Father in the name of Yeshua Ha Mashiach, Jesus Christ by his blood I plead forgiveness of the most heinous crimes-blasphemy - but it was not intentional, it is a sin I beg forgiveness, a sin of ignorance. Father please forgive me for the lust that I've been calling down upon myself and you know the rest of my story. I must write down the plan to remove these strongholds of lust and passion. I fully repent of this sin. I fully take responsibility even though I wasn't aware of what I was saying".

Wow... Looking back is always as they say 20/20 hindsight. I can see so clearly yet at the time I was blind and confused. The word I had been beating myself over was the word **"passion"**. It was my password for many things.

I spoke about my passion for the Lord and his passion for me in one of my songs and in my Love Tapestry poems. I spoke about our consummation in the poems but it was used in the context of being a spiritual consummation. However, the enemy at the time convinced me I was really speaking of a physical consummation and passion for the Lord. I came to this conclusion because something told me to look up the word passion and consummation in the dictionary.

I googled the definition and it spoke of a physical sexual relationship only. Why look to social media to understand. They can't appreciate the spiritual aspect which I was using. In all of this I listened to the enemy voices that battered me with this erroneous garbage. I allowed the enemy to convince me that I had committed blasphemy which is the unforgivable sin, sinning against the Holy Spirit. I begged God in this prayer over and over as though the BLOOD of Jesus could not alone wipe any stains away I imagined I had. If you say girl you were crazy, I would say yes, you are correct. Thanks to the Lord I know better now.

4/27/2015 COME LORD JESUS

Come Lord Jesus is a new song I would write. It had only been eight days since my incident at church. This ongoing battle continued to pursue me. In spite of the overwhelming, persistent onslaught of the enemy, I battled the spirits of lust, frustration, confusion and depression coming into my life. I forged ahead in my ongoing battle seeking complete deliverance. Unbelievably, I found a certain amount of peace and hope at the end of the day knowing victory was mine. I discerned the Lord and I were dancing a beautiful waltz at times but even better still, at other times a tango would be more like it. As I think about it, Jesus was leading the way of course at least most of the time. Otherwise I would not have made it that far. The waltz I find is a slow dance.

At times things seemed to be moving slow with no progress in sight of my battle. However, the tango is fast paced, making serious deliberate dance steps with quick turns and **kicking** movements. This dance would prove to be prophetic in many ways because of life situations taking quick turns as though coming out of nowhere. For certain, it was a time I was trying to **kick** the devil out of my life. As I look back at the time I didn't quite understand why it seemed at times I was making progress and others not so much. On this ordinary Monday afternoon I was missing the Lord something terrible. I could sense sometimes in my spirit (my heart) when he was near and even more so when not so near. This particular day my heart was truly yearning for him. As I sat there in my chair I reached for a pen and paper to start writing. I started singing the lyrics to a nice original melody and the song **"Come Lord Jesus"** was born. I love this song because it was the reawakening of my songwriting dreams and aspirations. I can't remember how long it had been since the last song I had written. I had only written a fragment of a song back in Dec 2014 or a poem but nothing in the way of songs during this time of my cleansing and serious spiritual battles. The Lord was steadily leading me down the path to this **Christ Directed CD** project titled **Dancing with the King of Kings** which was now in the making. **"Come Lord Jesus"** came along in God's **PERFECT TIMING.**

Some time later I went to an End Times Conference in Indianapolis. I made some wonderful new friends that I'm still in touch with through Facebook and email. Unfortunately, I had a horrible encounter on my way to Indianapolis for the conference that I will never forget. I traveled by Greyhound because I don't really like flying though I've flown a few times before. I made the mistake of using the bathroom on the bus and got stuck in there for two or three minutes, that seemed to be forever. It was pitch black, where I couldn't even see my hand. It reeked of urine and that strong sulfur smell filled my nostrils even though I tried covering my nose with my blouse. It was stronger than anything I had ever smelled in my life.

I was trying to figure out how to get out of there for several minutes fumbling with the lock. So it was even harder trying to unlock the lock and keep my nose covered at the same time. Finally I got out. I felt the presence of evil inside the bathroom and I came under severe spiritual attack while in Indianapolis at the conference. I told a group of brothers and sisters about what had happened at a gathering after the first day. They circled around me and prayed for me as everyone was looking scared and the sister that prayed for me made sure she didn't touch me. Nobody wanted any demons transferring to them. I couldn't blame them. I tried to enjoy the conference and for the most part I did but the spiritual attack dampened the experience for me. After the three day conference some of us stayed over at the house of a local sister for more fellowship.

That was an enjoyable time to fellowship with my brothers and sisters from different parts of the world even though I was sick, my blood pressure was extremely high. But I pressed in through the prayers. I had sung my song "Come Lord Jesus" impromptu to the sister in charge of the conference as we had breakfast together. I told her about my songs the Lord had been giving me. I asked her if I could share the song with everyone at the gathering. So she asked me to sing the song and judging by the reactions most if not all were blessed by this song. I presume it's because it speaks directly to the hearts of those longing for the Lord's return. Glory to God!!!

Come Lord Jesus

Lyrics and Melody by Faye A. Cross

Copyrighted 2015 © All rights reserved (BMI) Written: 27 April 2015 Revised: 27 Oct 2015

Verse 1:

Come Oh Come Lord Jesus, My Heart is longing for you, don't delay; Oh how I love you Jesus, at times you seem so far away

But I can see you through eyes of faith, at heaven's door we're face to face; Then you remind me, that you're not gone, I feel your heartbeat in this song

Bridge:

I'm really not so far away today

My Holy Spirit's with you always

Chorus:

Don't fret my child, in just awhile …you'll see me coming on the clouds; Don't fret my child, in just awhile… you will hear the trumpet sound

Verse 2:

Come Oh Come Lord Jesus, the world is getting darker day by day; Oh how I love you Jesus, your day of coming will be soon I pray; But I can hear you say don't give up, I'll be there for you when times get tough; Then you remind me, with you I'm strong, I hear your heartbeat in this song

Bridge:

I'm really not so far away today

My Holy Spirit's with you always REPEAT Chorus and Bridge

Chorus:

Don't fret my child, in just a while …you'll see me coming on the clouds; Don't fret my child, in just a while… you will hear the trumpet sound

Bridge: different melody

I'm really not so far away today,

My Holy Spirit's with you always (repeat) 3X

Repeat Chorus: 3X

June 2015

6/1/2015 WORD FROM THE LORD

This Monday morning journal entry was made after my prayer time with the Lord. He led me to Jeremiah 13 where the Lord had given Jeremiah a clear assignment to warn the people of God's coming wrath, that they would be taken into exile into Babylon because of their disobedience. I was now active on Facebook and writing for my Morning Manna with love blog.

6/6/2015 THE GLORY SONG

As you can see from the timeline many things had happened to try and discourage me to get me off track from this project which was still out of view at this point in time. However, God was calling me to produce a CD with songs leading us with the anticipation of the Lord's return to the actual celebration of the Bride and Bridegroom's Wedding.

I am focused now more than ever on doing the Lord's work. By this time I had written quite a few songs and my recordings were all done in acapella style. Some of my friends that I'd share them with would say to me, I sure would like to hear how that song sounds with music. At this point in time, the Lord directed me to purchase a keyboard. As I mentioned the CD project was not in clear view. I had no experience whatsoever of playing a keyboard or any musical instrument.

I had purchased a guitar once or twice over the years but I always ended up selling it after having it a few days realizing it was not something I was capable of learning. It was surprising that the Lord led me to purchase a keyboard. I knew He would have to teach me for sure and that He has been doing it little by little. One day I would like to get some professional lessons with a private tutor. I paid for an online course that I have failed to take advantage of. I need a real person to sit down with me and teach me. I regret wasting my money but it is what it is. In spite of having no lessons, I had no idea I would be composing beautiful instrumentals that reflect the beauty of the Lord and of heaven. At least they are beautiful to me. This Sunday afternoon I'm just starting to get acquainted with my new but used Yamaha 223 keyboard and the first complete composition the Lord leads me in to play.

I recorded and titled it **"The Glory Song"**. My first instrumental song sounded so beautiful to me in spite of the many sour notes I was hitting and the offbeat bad timing of my playing. I only heard what my heart was expressing to God and that was my immense love for Him. With all the imperfections I could hear a song and a melody that may someday become a recording. As I listened to it the only thing I could say was Glory to God and so I named it my Glory song. Glory!!!

July 2015

7/13/2015 BLESSED WITH A NEW SONG

Yeshua's Wedding Day

A little more than a month later after the instrumental Glory song I wrote a new song titled Yeshua's Wedding Day. It was one of the most beautiful songs to me that I had written thus far. To me the melody was just as special as the lyrics. I was really stretching out by recording myself singing in acapella and sharing it with a small group of friends on an email list.

I had shared some of my songs in the past with a few friends in my church bible study group setting but now I started sharing my recordings online. I received favorable feedback for the song from those who bothered to reply. I was more than happy with the Lord's gift to me of Yeshua's Wedding Day song, I was elated. I adore the name **YESHUA**, as much as I do the name **JESUS**. Some people sadly have a problem with that. I see it as a matter of semantics and spelling. The Jewish brethren who have embraced Jesus Christ as their Lord and Saviour just as we English speaking Gentiles have, have a right to call the Saviour of ALL mankind by His name in their native tongue. Jesus was Jewish so why shouldn't they call him by his Jewish Hebrew name.

Besides, I wrote a booklet titled, **"HOW JOY IS SALVATION'S NAME"** by which I break down this controversial issue of the pronunciation of the Lord's name. I discuss from a Gentile perspective because I believe God accepts the name of our Savior in whatever our native tongue or language is.

Yeshua's Wedding Day by Faye A. Cross

All rights reserved © Copyright 2015-2017

Prophetic Song based on Matthew 25:1-13, Revelation 19:9, Revelation 5:6, 8-10, Psalm 2:9-12, Revelation 3:12, Ephesians 5:23-27, Song of Songs 1:3, 2:4, 4:7, 6:4, Matthew 16: 1-4, Matthew 24: 29-30, Isaiah 55:10-11 Written: **7/13/2015**

Verse 1

Yeshua(Jesus) will someday, soon take his bride away

He's excited, delighted to see her face when they embrace

Her light is shining bright in a world as dark as midnight

She's been waiting, anticipating her time will come to Kiss the Son

Chorus:

Holy, holy is the lamb that was slain for, for all unrighteous men. Holy Matrimony, sanctioned by His blood and Word. Our hearts will now be more than stirred, all the hearts that belong to Him

Verse 2

The wedding day will come for **Yeshua (Jesus)** is the Holy One

He's excited, delighted, His banner covers her with LOVE

She stands in holiness, she left the world without regret

She's waiting, anticipating to take on His new sacred name

Repeat Chorus:

2nd Chorus:

Holy Hoooooly is the lamb that was slain for all unrighteous men; Holy Matrimony, sanctioned by His blood and Word, our hearts will now be more than stirred; All the hearts that belong to Him

Verse 3:

Signs set in the sky ordained by God revealing time

He's faithful, so careful to keep his Word of promises we've heard; The foolish didn't see, they missed the day and hour of the thief; They'll be crying, and dying a senseless loss at a great cost

Repeat Chorus:

Repeat 2nd Chorus:

7/16/2015 LAMB OF GOD

(CROSS UPON CALVARY)

I recorded a song I titled **"Lamb of God" (Cross Upon Calvary)** on the night of July 16, 2015 as the Holy Spirit led me to play on my new keyboard. The spiritual chords I play in this song have special meaning which I write about in great detail in my book, **"Dance with the King of Kings (Heaven's Perfect Chord) C MAJOR"** This was my first keyboard which at the time I'd had for around a month. This night, the Lord led me to practice playing a couple of other songs He was teaching me earlier that night. I was quite tired when I finally went to bed around midnight. As I was trying to go to sleep, all of a sudden I received a vision in my spirit which kind of stunned me. I had a vision of the Lord lying on the ground and I sensed his face was severely beaten and bruised.

It wasn't anything like some visions I have heard described where they see in panavision and technicolor. No, this was in my spirit. I felt and sensed deep darkness as though I was there with him experiencing the spiritual darkness he had been thrust into. My room was naturally dark because I had turned the lights off to go to sleep. But this was more than normal darkness. I soon realized this was actually a vision of him as he laid on the ground having been taken down from the cross. *This prompted me to begin writing,* **"Lay Him Down".**

I was seeing the Lamb of God after having been slain lying on the ground before he was prepared for burial. Immediately after getting this vision in my spirit I was prompted by the Holy Spirit to go back to the keyboard which was right next to my bed. I dragged myself up, not knowing what I would be playing but I just started playing thinking I would be playing again what I had played earlier. But no, this really dark sound came out of the keyboard because the Lord led me to the lowest register of notes on the keyboard, **C Major** and **D Minor** for the first few seconds of the song. Then I moved over to somewhat higher notes of **G Major** and **A Minor.** I came to understand how a song can start out sad but end with an uplifting sound. For the most part the song was beautiful though appropriately very sad, and mournful in parts. Poignant in the richness of its true essence because in the end it was mysteriously uplifting.

When I listened to the playback, I could hear angelic voices singing, **"hallelujah"** exactly 8 times. After that, I could hear them say, **"standing on a hill", "standing on a mount" and "coming to the earth",** each 8 times as well. This is done throughout the entire song. I can still hear it today, it always sounds the same. So far, no one hears it but me. I was a little taken back hearing the angelic voices singing **"hallelujah"** after all, I was feeling so sad about Jesus' face being beaten and bruised. He died such a painful cruel death for us. The song initially sounded like coming from a dungeon or deep pit.

But then the Lord started speaking to my spirit (my heart). He helped me to understand that though the Lamb of God was sacrificed and died a cruel death, the end result was victory because he rose from the dead, from the deep pit of hell. The end justifies the means to a new beginning of life. Now I see that the Lord was allowing me to experience what Jesus experienced being in a spiritual dungeon surrounded by the enemy. We know he felt abandoned by the Father and understandably so.

The Father stepped back allowing the enemy to crucify the Lord. Though Jesus was plunged into the pits of hell so that we would have life, he was not abandoned there. He was raised to life after 3 days and 3 nights in the dungeon which was his grave. Glory to the Father! Compare Psalm 88:6 and Acts 2:27, 31-32 These truths uplifted my spirit as I was reminded that it was necessary that he suffer on the cross as painful as it was. Suddenly I heard a new melody with a different sound and meaning which is born out of the lyrics of the song **"Lay Him Down"** titled **"The Glory Arises"**.

*[Psalm 88:6 NIV] 6 You have **put me in the lowest pit, in the darkest depths**.*

*[Acts 2:27, 31-32 KJV] 27 Because thou **wilt not leave my soul in hell**, neither wilt thou suffer thine Holy One to see corruption. ... 31 He seeing this before spake of the resurrection of Christ, that his soul was not left in hell, neither his flesh did see corruption. 32 This Jesus hath God raised up, whereof we all are witnesses.*

THE MAKING OF LAY HIM DOWN"

The main verses and chorus of the song **"Lay Him Down"** came out of my vision that I saw and described in my opening remarks about the making of **"Lamb of God" (The Cross on Calvary)** instrumental. In the vision I could see and feel in my spirit a vision of the Lord's face as he laid on the ground after having been beaten and bruised. From this vision the Holy Spirit led me to write the lyrics with a new fresh melody to go along with them. Somehow I imagined the conversation between the rich man Joseph of Arimathaea who was given the body of Jesus to bury. One account speaks of Nicodemus being there along with Joseph and the soldiers when they asked for Jesus' body to be taken down off of the cross or from the tree. Some of the scriptures say the body was handed over to Joseph implying the soldiers took Him down and another says Joseph took the body down. In either case I imagined hearing Joseph giving instructions to the soldiers to take down the one wearing the crown or telling them he was there to take down the body of the one with the crown of thorns. Especially since there were two men crucified with Jesus, thus referring to the crown of thorns the soldiers had put on Jesus' head.

I don't think my thinking is out of line nor unreasonable to imagine the whole scenario that took place there on Calvary. But I admit that is simply my imagination. I believe the Holy Spirit leads me in my thinking.

Though the crown of thorns were put together to mock Jesus, we know those thorns symbolized the real crown Jesus would wear after being resurrected. For he's wearing a crown now as he sits on his throne at the right hand of the Father in heaven. He is waiting to soon return to the earth to rule and reign as King of Kings and Lord of Lords as He now reigns in heaven.

Lay Him Down *Melody/Lyrics by* **Faye A. Cross (Inspired by the Holy Spirit)** *8/7/2015 Copyright © 2016 All rights reserved*

Verse 1

Unrecognizable, his face was torn apart

His face was badly bruised, Covered with scars and marred

When at the ninth hour, he seemed to lose power

He cried my God, why? His spirit left, he died

But on the third day he rose up from the dead

When Mary looked for him, She saw him up ahead

And now to her surprise, Her Savior was alive

She watched him pay the cost, To die upon the CROSS

Chorus:

Lay him down, From the cross take him down, He's the one wearing a crown of thorns on his head, but now he's dead; Lay him down, From the cross take him down,

He'll only spend 3 days and nights in the ground; He'll rise forever crowned; Lay him down, …. repeat

Verse 2

Jesus Christ the King, mistreated Holy One

His time will come to rule God let your kingdom come

He'll come again now.., he'll stand on holy ground

To save Jerusalem as enemies surround

He'll strike the nations rule with an iron rod

His day of wrath must come restoring peace and love

It's what he did for you and what he did for me

He hung upon the cross, until his spirit would leave

<u>Chorus:</u>

Lay him down, From the cross take him down, He's the one

wearing a crown of thorns on his head, but now he's dead; Lay him down, From the cross take him down,

He'll only spend 3 days and nights in the ground; He'll rise forever crowned; Lay him down, …. repeat

Here are the scriptures to support the lyrics of "Lay Him Down".

Jesus body is turned over to Joseph of Arimathaea

(Matthew 27:57-60 KJV) 57 When the even was come, there came a rich man of Arimathaea, named Joseph, who also himself was Jesus' disciple: 58 He went to Pilate, and begged the body of Jesus. Then Pilate commanded the body to be delivered. 59 And when Joseph had taken the body, he wrapped it in a clean linen cloth, 60 And laid it in his own new tomb, which he had hewn out in the rock: and he rolled a great stone to the door of the sepulchre, and departed.

(Mark 15:43-46 KJV) 43 Joseph of Arimathaea, an honourable counsellor, which also waited for the kingdom of God, came, and went in boldly unto Pilate, and craved the body of Jesus. 44 And Pilate marvelled if he were already dead: and calling [unto him] the centurion, he asked whether he had been any while dead. 45 And when he knew [it] of the centurion, he gave the body to Joseph. 46 And he bought fine linen, and took him down, and wrapped him in the linen, and laid him in a sepulchre which was hewn out of a rock, and rolled a stone unto the door of the sepulchre. *(Luke 23:50-53 KJV)* 50 And, behold, [there was] a man named Joseph, a counsellor; [and he was] a good man, and a just: 51 (The same had not consented to the counsel and deed of them;) [he was] of Arimathaea, a city of the Jews: who also himself waited for the kingdom of God. 52 This [man] went unto Pilate, and begged the body of Jesus. 53 And he took it down, and wrapped it in linen, and laid it in a sepulchre that was hewn in stone, wherein never man before was laid.

(John 19:2, 5, 38-41 KJV) 2 And the soldiers platted a crown of thorns, and put [it] on his head, and they put on him a purple robe, ...

5 Then came Jesus forth, wearing the crown of thorns, and the purple robe. And [Pilate] saith unto them, Behold the man! ... 38 And after this Joseph of Arimathaea, being a disciple of Jesus, but secretly for fear of the Jews, besought Pilate that he might take away the body of Jesus: and Pilate gave [him] leave. He came therefore, and took the body of Jesus.

At the ninth hour Jesus died

(**Luke 23:44-46 KJV**) 44 And it was about the sixth hour, and there was a darkness over all the earth until **the ninth hour**. 45 And the sun was darkened, and the veil of the temple was rent in the midst. 46 And when **Jesus had cried** with a loud voice, he said, **Father, into thy hands I commend my spirit: and having said thus, he gave up the ghost.**

(**Matthew 27:45-51 KJV**) 45 Now from the sixth hour there was darkness over all the land unto the ninth hour. 46 And **about the ninth hour Jesus cried** with a loud voice, saying, Eli, Eli, lama sabachthani? that is to say, **My God, my God, why hast thou forsaken me?** 47 Some of them that stood there, when they heard [that], said, This [man] calleth for Elias.

48 And straightway one of them ran, and took a spunge, and filled [it] with vinegar, and put [it] on a reed, and gave him to drink. 49 The rest said, Let be, let us see whether Elias will come to save him. 50 **Jesus, when he had cried again with a loud voice, yielded up the ghost.** 51 And, behold, the veil of the temple was rent in twain from the top to the bottom; and the earth did quake, and the rocks rent;

Mary meets the Lord on the road

(**Matthew 28:6-9 KJV**) 6 He is not here: for he is risen, as he said. Come, see the place where the Lord lay. 7 And **go quickly, and tell his disciples that he is risen from the dead;** and, behold, he goeth before you into Galilee; there shall ye see him: lo, I have told you. 8 And they departed quickly from the sepulchre with fear and great joy; and did run to bring his disciples word. 9 And **as they went to tell his disciples,** *behold, Jesus met them, saying, All hail. And they came and held him by the feet, and worshipped him.*

Jesus will rule from Jerusalem bringing peace

(Zec 14:4, 8-9, 11, 16, 20 KJV) 4 And his feet shall stand in that day upon the mount of Olives, which [is] before Jerusalem on the east, and the mount of Olives shall cleave in the midst thereof toward the east and toward the west, [and there shall be] a very great valley; and half of the mountain shall remove toward the north, and half of it toward the south. ...

*8 And it shall be in that day, [that] living waters shall go out from Jerusalem; half of them toward the former sea, and half of them toward the hinder sea: in summer and in winter shall it be. 9 **And the LORD shall be king over all the earth: in that day shall there be one LORD, and his name one.** ... 11 **And [men] shall dwell in it, and there shall be no more utter destruction; but Jerusalem shall be safely inhabited.** ...*

16 And it shall come to pass, [that] every one that is left of all the nations which came against Jerusalem shall even go up from year to year to worship the King, the LORD of hosts, and to keep the feast of tabernacles. ... 20 In that day shall there be upon the bells of the horses, HOLINESS UNTO THE LORD; and the pots in the LORD'S house shall be like the bowls before the altar.

*(**Rev 19:15-16 KJV**) 15 And out of his mouth goeth a sharp sword, that with it he should smite the nations: and he shall rule them with a rod of iron: and he treadeth the winepress of the fierceness and wrath of Almighty God. 16 And he hath on [his] vesture and on his thigh a name written, KING OF KINGS, AND LORD OF LORDS*

7/19/2015 BRIDEGROOM'S HEART

Today was an unusual Sunday evening. The Lord surprised me as I was resting and relaxing in bed. All of a sudden I could hear him singing a song to me in my spirit. It was so loving. Jesus is really funny and playful which I love about him. I wrote the lyrics down and recorded the song titled **"Bridegroom's Heart".** He told me the song was for his bride so I shared it with some friends on Facebook. I must say today as I'm writing this book that I miss the Lord so much. It's like there is a silence now in heaven. I have His Holy Spirit for sure but I don't have the conversations with him as I've had in the past. It's been awhile. That's why I love these songs so much because they speak deeply to my heart and soul of my profound love for the Lord. Moreover, they speak to me of the love he has for me. There's no love like the love of God. **Update**: At the time I wrote this in July 2015, I wasn't familiar with the scripture that says, God sings over us. I was pleasantly surprised to find it. Praise the Lord!!! *Read Zephaniah 3:17*

Bridegroom's Heart by Faye A. Cross

Copyright 2015 All rights reserved (BMI) Written: 7/19/2015

Verse 1

I love you bride and you know it, know it

You'll never ever be alone again

You will have to believe

when it's hard to see that you're my reality

Chorus:

I want to give you my heart, give you my heart right now

I know I'm your first love any how

Your heart has spoken to me

by your own decree to always abide in me

Bridge:

That's why you will find my wings you can hide anytime

That's why you will find my wings you can hide anytime

Just rest in me and you will see there's freedom

freedom from all the cares of the world, there's freedom for you

Verse 2

I love you bride and you know it, know it

I want to be with you right now

You will have to believe

when it's hard to see that you're my reality

August 2015

8/7/2015 THERE'S A WIND BLOWING

On this day I made my first composition and video recording of **"There's a Wind Blowing" Part 1.** I see it as one of my first decent sounding instrumentals I had done thus far. Over time the Lord has led me in creating many renditions of this song with different melody and voice patterns. As I listened to the playback I could hear the words there's a wind blowing and that shaped the overall concept of the lyrics for this song.

There's a Wind Blowing (Inspired by the Holy Spirit)

Lyrics, melody and music arrangement by **Faye A. Cross**

Copyright © 2015 All rights reserved (BMI) Written: 8/7/2015

Verse1
There's a wind blowing your way

It's bringing blessings and favor today

There's a way that is righteous and true to deliver you

Abide in me the living word and pray your way through

Bridge:
Unbelievable the fire of your zeal ...Praying before the altar you kneel; So believable, the perfumes of heaven reel

Inconceivable! Your faith the enemy can't steal

Verse 2
There's a wind blowing from the windows of heaven over you today; Heaven knows when to send it your way...

Living waters from heaven flowing everyday

The windows of heaven are opened over you today

Chorus:
Let the winds blow...let the winds flow from heaven to down here below; Let the winds blow...let the winds flow from heaven to down here below

There's a dove from above to deliver all my love

He will stay with you to comfort you until the day I come

September 2015

9/15/2015 STAYING BUSY

September was not a busy month for making music because I was busy working on my blog "Morning Manna with Love". And I was also revamping and editing my other website, a devotional called "Hope Devotions". In spite of all the things I had on my plate, I was able to find time to record a couple of new instrumentals, **"Lilies"** and **"Wedding Song March"**.

October 2015

10/16/2015 YESHUA'S WEDDING DAY

SINGING AT APC CHURCH

I decided to do something that was out of the box for me, to sing in a talent show at church. I wanted to share my song, Yeshua's Wedding Day, which I had written 3 months earlier. The purpose of the talent show was to raise funds for the youth ministry's missions fund. Right before the time for me to go on and sing, they had an intermission to give out a few door prizes. They knew I was quite nervous so they let me relax through most of the show leaving me next to last to sing.

God was answering an unspoken prayer in my heart. My door prize was a flashing mouth light with rainbow colors. This was a clear sign from heaven's throne room for me. For one I am a child at heart and this clearly showed me the Lord's beautiful sense of humor which I had come to expect of him and love. We had a good chuckle inside of my heart over the mouth light and this whole occasion. But also it said to me, daughter I've given you this song to sing and the lyrics are a light in your mouth.

Let your light shine my daughter. Earlier in the day when I was practicing the song in my bedroom, a sweet aroma came into my room as the Lord spoke to my spirit. He said that the song would bless people at the church function and some would tell me how much the song meant to them. I love it when I can see the Lord's fingerprints all over everything. Several people did tell me how much they liked the song. One sister told me she wanted to get the lyrics, saying, "You need to get that song played on the radio." Another sister told me," I was singing right along with you". That made my heart glad. I give God the glory. It's all about him. I have a short version on the CD **"Dancing with the King of Kings"** but hopefully I will get to record the full version for the website. You can find the lyrics on page 171-172.

November 2015

11/17/2015 JOURNAL ENTRY AND WORD

You are beautiful my daughter. You are here in heaven with me now. You look so beautiful in your gown. It is perfect on you. Fine clean linen. Spotless. You are perfect in ME.

I received this word after calling out to **Yeshua (Jesus)** because the spiritual warfare was intense. All evening I tried playing the music for the wedding the Lord has put in my heart. On the playback after recording the music the sound was muffled and not clear and the volume was so low I could barely hear it. A clear sign the enemy does not want this music to go forth. This music I have dedicated to my Lord and Saviour, my bridegroom Yeshua Ha Maschiach (Jesus Christ the Messiah). I'm just a humble servant of the Lord. I don't know how to play the keyboard but the Holy Spirit leads me in these songs.

They are simple songs in delivery because I am not a professional keyboardist. However the Lord inspires me to play anyway. Under normal circumstances I would never share this music with anyone knowing how flawed it is yet I know it's about HIM and he assures me it will bless all those who belong to him, all who long for his coming. I pray now and call out to the Lord that he would cover me and bind the enemy so that I can produce the music he so lovingly has given to me to share with the world. It is about preparing hearts for the King of Kings and Lord of Lords.

SONGS WRITTEN THE WEEK OF THANKSGIVING

11/19/2015 - There's a wind blowing (2 new renditions)

11/20/2015 - Dance with the King - Instrumental

11/22/2015 - Golden Sunrise - Instrumental

11/24/2015 - You Changed My Whole Life -melody and lyrics / Heaven Singing Over Me - Instrumental

11/26/2015 - Beholding El Shaddai (at the throne) - Instrumental

11/27/2015 - Lion of Judah - Instrumental / Dancing with the King II/Come Enter the Gate medley - melody and lyrics

11/28/2015 - You are Worthy - melody and lyrics

I give the Lord all praise, glory and honor !!!! Halleluyah!

11/19/2015 THERE'S A WIND BLOWING - Part 2

The first rendition of **"There's a wind blowing"** was composed on August 6, 2015. I have found that several of the instrumentals are like songs in progress. The Lord gives it to me in bits and pieces. I find it fascinating as I learn to play the keyboard that I get to learn from Jesus, the great teacher himself through His Holy Spirit. There are many voice instruments on my keyboard to experiment with.

Exactly seven days before Thanksgiving day, I was led to play some new melodies and chords for "There's a wind blowing". In the end I hope to take the good bits and pieces to make one good complete song. In spite of the attacks, the Lord gave me beautiful songs for the **Dancing with the King CD.**

11/20/2015 DANCE W/THE KING-INSTRUMENTAL

What a joyful sound to my ears when I listen to the instrumental song **"Dance with the King" (DWTK).** It reflects all of creation celebrating at the wedding banquet of the Lamb and his bride. The Lord not only blessed me with this cheerful jubilant song but He also led me in creating several songs this week that may be on the CD, website or both.

11/22/2015 GOLDEN SUNRISE - INSTRUMENTAL

On Sunday, the 22nd of November, I was led by the Holy Spirit to play a melody to classic Cuban beat and sound. As I'm writing this I see me and the Lord dancing. It's a happy melody with a fast beat fit for lots of twirling. I can see rows of people twirling along the river of life dancing on the golden streets of heaven to this melody. I titled it **"Golden Sunrise"**. Why? Because I imagine the timing of the sunrise as the beginning of the day. When we first get to heaven it will be like the sun rising after being on an earth full of darkness.

The sunrise is a beautiful time of the day, though the sun never sets in heaven. I envision a golden haze overhead as we're all dancing along the river of life and other streets of gold in heaven. HalleluYAH! Listen, I hope it transports you to heaven. Imagine yourself dancing with your favorite person. Glory to God!!!

11/24/2015 HEAVEN SINGING OVER ME- MUSIC

Two days before Thanksgiving I played the instrumental **"Heaven Singing Over Me"**. This **instrumental composition** is so beautiful to me as it reflects the beauty of heaven. It is a slow song with a beat, No. 5 called Adria on my keyboard. As you know the number five represents God's **GRACE** and maybe that's why I am so fond of this beat. I used it in several songs featured on the **DWTK CD** . I love the simplicity of the undertones of the beat.

It's not overpowering, loud or base. It's simply perfect. The Lord led me in playing the strings voice in the higher octave range for the melody. When I listened to the playback it felt like heaven was singing over me. I feel the Lord's love and favor in a special way as I listen. I've tried playing this song again and I haven't been able to duplicate it yet. Maybe someday but for now, I'm content to listen to the recording which captures the anointing of God's spirit being poured out in this melody. Thank you Lord. To you be all the Glory!!!

11/24/2015 YOU CHANGED MY WHOLE LIFE

Tuesday was a good day as I wrote another song, this time with lyrics which I call my anthem **"You Changed My Whole Life"**. The Lord led me in writing the lyrics as he brought to the surface my heartfelt appreciation of his love, protection and deliverance. The lyrics speak for themselves. It was a smooth melody I heard in my spirit as I started singing acapella working out the melody before playing it on the keyboard. I've recorded two versions with different melodic beats, a pop melody and jazzy. I tend to favor the jazz version but I like the pop version as well.

You Changed My Whole Life

Melody and lyrics by **Faye A. Cross**
Copyright 2015-2016 © All Rights Reserved (BMI)
Written: Nov 24, 2015/ 1:11 AM ~ *Inspired by the Holy Spirit*

Verse 1
Jesus you will always be my light in the dark, a candle within my heart. And never will a day go by, I don't call your name... without you I'd go insane

Chorus:
I cried to thee purify me, repenting through the night

GRACE covered me, delivered me, Jesus you came, you saved my life Jesus you came, you changed my whole life (repeat)

Verse 2
I think about you day and night Jesus, You're always upon my heart. And never will a day go by without your love, my dove from up above

Repeat Chorus

Bridge:
In the middle of the night I had to call on you
You changed my life ...You changed my life Jesus
The enemy attacked my mind, said I wouldn't make it through
You changed my life....You changed my life Jesus
But I kept hearing in my heart, the living Word of truth
You changed my life....You changed my life Jesus
Say, I am there with you, you're not alone.. I've come to rescue you, You saved my life, you saved my life Jesus.....

I will always be thankful and grateful that you are my friend. I will always cherish that what we have will never come to an end

11/26/2015 BEHOLDING EL SHADDAI-MUSIC

On Thanksgiving Day, I followed the Holy Spirit's lead as usual and recorded a song titled **"Beholding El Shaddai (at the throne)**. I remember when I first started playing the chords to this instrumental composition some months earlier and the Lord brought it all together for me in a classical waltz that exuded His glory, power, and holiness. The Lord would not stop blessing me, leading me with more instrumental songs. As we continued to dance together His favor and grace poured out in abundance overflowing in me.

11/27/2015 THE LION OF JUDAH/INSTRUMENTAL

Today He led me in another new instrumental composition that I titled **"The Lion of Judah"**. It seemed to be the appropriate title to me because that's what I see and feel in my spirit when I listen to it.

11/27/2015 DANCE WITH THE KING (LYRICS)

The Holy Spirit had led me in composing the instrumental **DWTK** and a week later, the day after Thanksgiving I penned the lyrics to the instrumental **"Dance with the King"**. I will always know my God is perfect knowing the song was incomplete without the lyrics. Now it's **perfect and complete**. Within a week, the Lord had given me eight songs though counting **Dance With The King/Come Enter the Gate** as a two song medley, nine songs would be more accurate.

THE MAKING OF "DANCE WITH THE KING" I/II

To God be all the Glory, for He alone deserves all the glory, honor and praise! I get excited talking about these songs. I have to say this song became my go to song when writing sometimes. It reminds me of what I believe it will be like when we are raptured to be with the Lord in heaven, our glorious King. I perceive the deep love and compassion stored in the heart of **Jesus (Yeshua)** for us.

I can even sense the Lord's anticipation as I perceive the immense joy, peace and happiness that He must be feeling as He waits for the Father's signal to come for His bride church. And are these not the same emotions that fill the hearts of His faithful bride church as she waits for her bridegroom. I feel so many emotions when listening to the melody and lyrics of **"Come Enter the Gate"**. Oh, how beautiful the realm of eternity will be. I'm forever grateful and thankful to **Jesus (Yeshua)** and our heavenly Father **YAHWEH (Jehovah)** for giving me the secure hope of dwelling with them for all eternity. How about you?

Read Hebrews 6:19-20 and Philippians 3:20

Time will stand still as we enter the dominion of the King of Kings realms of eternity beginning with heaven ending on earth.

It will be a time of great jubilation and celebration as the Father celebrates with us along with all of heaven. Because it's the Father's wedding as well. His Son is glorified forever to the glory of the Father. He reigns in royal majesty. The best part is we get to reign along with him. How we each get to participate in that remains to be seen. Glory to our Lord and King forever. HalleluYAH!

[Rev 20:6 NIV] 6 Blessed and holy are those who share in the first resurrection. The second death has no power over them, but they will be priests of God and of Christ and will **reign with him for a thousand years**. *[Rev 5:10 NIV] 10 You have made them to be a* **kingdom and priests** *to serve our God, and* **they will reign on the earth**.*"*

I am excited to tell you about the making of **"Dance with the King I & II" (Come Enter the Gate)**. First of all I had no idea I would be writing and composing a new song on Friday, November 20, 2015 which is the day I played this song on the keyboard for the first time. Never had I ever heard this melody before in my entire life but I started hearing it in my spirit the night before when the Lord started giving me the first part. I am thankful and grateful that I would come to write the lyrics exactly 7 days later on November 27, 2015, the day after Thanksgiving. It occurred to me after I recorded myself playing the song that I would not be able to reproduce any of these instrumental songs exactly as I have recorded them because I wing it. What I mean is I pray before I push the record button and start playing as the Holy Spirit takes over. He leads me to the notes and controls the beat pattern. Well, most of the time when I am being led by His Spirit. Many times the enemy has come in to frustrate me, attempting to sabotage this whole project. I probably told you this before but at times they would mess with my voice where I couldn't sing, my voice would constantly crack and sound awful. I know I'm not the best singer but it was so blatantly obvious to me when the opposition was present. Yet I never gave up. No song will ever sound exactly the same as the original recording. My prayer is that when I play the songs over and over again, eventually I will learn to play them as close as possible to the original version. I've always disliked it when I hear someone singing or playing a song I like hearing on the radio and in person it sounds totally different. Now I understand why, because it's somewhat difficult to recapture the original unless you learn it by practicing the song over and over again.

However, I must admit that I kind of like improvising as I go along. It adds a certain element of creativity and new flavor to enhance the original. Improvisation is always so much fun as I work with the Holy Spirit, He inspires me as He leads me along to play. By now you know that all of the songs have special meaning behind them. All songwriters would agree with me and say their songs always have a special meaning behind them. What is unique about my songs on this CD is the fact that some of the songs, though not all, have meanings connected to the CHORDS and melody NOTES I play led by the Holy Spirit. I've written about how and why the letters of the chords are reflected in the lyrics of the song. Someday I hope to tell you all about it, if the Lord is willing. **(I'm praying for discernment and wisdom regarding a book).** I have come to know the Holy Spirit by the essence of his character traits of pure love, joy, beauty, holiness and gentleness all interwoven inside a soft fluffy white pillow that I can rest my head on. I confess that I practiced a little dancing with the Lord in my heart of hearts as I listened to the instrumental. As I imagined myself dancing with Him, at one point I sensed His tangible presence through the Holy Spirit. It was a happy joyful moment for me!!! As mentioned earlier, there are two parts to **"Dance with the King"**. Part I is instrumental. Part II carries the instrumental melody with anointed lyrics weaving a glorious tapestry of our King's soon coming millennial reign. The accompanying beat used is a Viennese waltz beat, perfect for the chords I play on the strings voice of the keyboard.

[Psalm 45:8 NIV] *8 All your robes are fragrant with myrrh and aloes and cassia; from* **palaces adorned with ivory the music of the strings makes you glad**.

Psalm 45:8 cited above, tells us that the Lord loves the strings and He fancies adornments of ivory. What a combination, ivory and strings! The prophetic fulfillment of this scripture is for our time indeed! The end times...a time such as this. I saw this scripture come to life in our day and time because today we can play a **stringed instrument** sound on some

keyboards equipped with a sound engine holding many stringed instruments like violins, harps, and cellos along with other instrument sounds and voices.

These keyboards can be likened to a **"palace adorned with ivory"** for the keyboard **houses "stringed" instruments with ebony and ivory keys.** Each time I play the strings voice on my keyboard I sense in my spirit that I am making the Lord's heart glad with strings as it states at *Psalm 45:8*. If you also play the keys, you may be especially glad to know this if you didn't realize it before. It's such a joy to play these songs for Him. To God be the glory!!! I love it!

RECORDING CHALLENGES

The morning I recorded **"Dance with the King I"** instrumental melody in my bedroom, the enemy kept trying to interfere with distracting noises. Taking advantage of the fact I was not recording in a professional sound proof environment, several times I had to start over. Why? Because an airplane flew overhead twice. I've been living here 7 years and never heard a plane flying over. Sometimes there are helicopters that fly overhead that can be disturbing but never planes. From my vantage point at times I have seen planes off in the distance that appear to be headed towards the airport but their course never ever led them over my apartment except this one day. It happened twice, two planes within ten minutes. They were so loud both times it ruined my recording.

Also because my apartment is situated next to a room where lots of people go in and out, at times they would make louder than usual distracting noises. Moreover, the day I recorded there were also some workers on our premises and they just so happen to be working right outside my apartment window using a loud buzz saw. You can hear it in the beginning of the song because I got tired of stopping and starting, it seemed they would start up whenever I would start to record. I decided enough was enough and left the buzz saw sound in and actually it sounds kind of cool. Only I know it is a buzz saw but now you know too. Nothing can stop what God has ordained us to do. He takes what the enemy meant for bad and makes it for our good. Here are the lyrics for Dance with the King II (Come Enter the Gate). It is on the CD and website.

DANCE WITH THE KING II/COME ENTER THE GATE SONG MEDLEY

Lyrics and Melody by **Faye A. Cross Inspired by Holy Spirit**

Verse 1

Come Enter the Gate, the Almighty Comes Enthroned

We'll dance and sing forever, for He's worthy alone

Come Enter the Gate, you end time warriors

Sons of God follow the King, dance in your royal armor

Chorus

I wanna dance with you my King, wanna tell you everything
May I dance with you my King? for this day I've often dreamed
I wanna sing you a song, as we dance along, the river, the river of life; And as we reminisce our story, I'll give you ALL the GLORY, it will be a pure delight…. to see your eyes smiling bright, as you tell me, there's no more midnight, no no, no no

Bridge

Bow down, (pause) bow down (pause) to the King of Kings (repeat) Banquet doors open wide for HIS REDEEMED!

Bow down, (pause) bow down (pause) to the King of Kings (repeat) Come enter His Glory Beloved and REDEEMED!

Music Interlude

Verse 2

Clap Dance and Enter, Jerusalem behold

We'll Dance For Abba Father, on pavements of Gold

Come Enter the Gate, the King of Glory awaits

Sons of God in perfect stride, dance for honor and glory

Repeat Chorus

Verse 3

Come Enter the Gate, my God and Bridegroom Descends

On Earth he'll reign forever, as Earth's Glory Begins

Come Enter the Gate, Faithful Army Chosen

Gone's the Beast and Devil, Fate of Anti-Christ settled

Repeat Chorus

Verse 4

Clap Dance and Enter Dance For Abba my soul

in New Jerusalem, we'll dance on streets of Gold

Come Enter the Gate, the King of Glory awaits

Sons of God in perfect stride dance for the King

Repeat Chorus and Bridge

Come Enter the Gate

Come enter the gate, come enter the gate ...come enter the gate , come enter the gate, come enter the gate, the King of glory awaits for His Bride. Come enter the gate,, won't you dance along Father's side...will you be there, will you be there to see the love of your life, beloved and redeemed of Christ will you be there? we're all invited to the marriage supper of the Lamb, tell all the poor and needy, we're all invited by the great I AM...come enter the gate, come enter the gate, the King of glory awaits for His bride, will you be there, will you there, to see the love of your life the redeemer Jesus Christ, we're all invited, all invited to the marriage supper of the Lamb of the great I AM.. , I hope you'll be there...I hope to be there too, will you pray for me and I'll pray you...we just have to be there to see our Lord, He's been so faithful, so faithful and true....I just love Him, from the depths of my heart and we each have a part to play, in this story right from the start, God knew we would have a place in His heart, and now's the time of the end my friend, when God would do away with all suffering and sin, come enter the gate, come enter the gate

11/28/2015 YOU ARE WORTHY

The eighth song was the appropriate song to begin my day with. I was awakened early in the morning around 5am, to hear in my spirit the words "you are worthy" being said over and over. I wrote and sang the lyrics within ten minutes of hearing it in my spirit. Soon after writing the lyrics to the song **"You Are Worthy"** the enemy tried to defile those words to the song the Holy Spirit had given me. I recorded myself singing the song within a few hours and played it on my computer. The enemy planted on my computer screen a large dark shadowed male sex organ moving in a sexual way. Sadly, it's not surprising that the enemy would plant the male sex organ on my video. The world worships it just as it was in ancient times.

Some bible scholars have said that there were idols made and worshiped in this form and it was a way for them to turn their nose up to God knowing how he felt about the sexual sins and abominations done in the land. Pornography is probably the number one search item on the internet. We live in a world where sex is worshiped to the point that even the children are learning to be preoccupied with their sexual identity with the opposite sex.

We can see pics of little girls dressed inappropriately for their age wearing makeup on their little otherwise innocent faces. I've seen children encouraged as young as 8 and 9 for dancing in a sexually suggestive manner dressed in adult costumes and makeup all under the pretense of ballroom dancing. It's the pervasive spirit of lust that is prevailing in the world and that same spirit I rebuked in the name of Jesus. I had to delete the video because the sexual image was planted on the video but the song will stand as a part of my testimony through all eternity, as it says, **YOU ARE WORTHY JESUS**!

[Rev 4:11 NIV] 11 "You are worthy, our Lord and God, to receive glory and honor and power, for you created all things, and by your will they were created and have their being." Rev 5:9 NIV] 9 And they sang a new song, saying: "You are worthy to take the scroll and to open its seals, because you were slain, and with your blood you purchased for God persons from every tribe and language and people and nation.

He is worthy because He delivered me from sexual sin though the enemy wants to keep me in bondage to it. It wants to keep reminding me of my past. I've learned through the Holy Spirit and my dance with the King that I am free from sin and no longer in bondage to my past sins. I may slip up from time to time out of weakness but that is not the same as willful sin without repentance. Read *Romans 7:6-7* Praise God! Although there is freedom from the law as the apostle Paul says, that does not mean that the law of God is no longer of any benefit to us.

It is the law that tells us what is and isn't right in God's eye. I love the law of God because I can better understand the God I love and serve. The best part of all God has written his law on the Christian's heart. The law of love is what God is wanting to impress upon our hearts. He is LOVE. The Holy Spirit helped me to appreciate the true meaning behind our freedom in Christ Jesus. We are now free from the law of sin and death because Christ kept the law perfectly where we couldn't and therefore he nailed sin and death to the cross. Now no longer under the bondage of sin or death, we can live captive to Christ, walking in the Spirit of Christ. When we walk in the Spirit, we are walking in the power of Christ by the grace of God. As we are led by the Spirit, we manifest as the true sons of God that is if we are walking in the Spirit, if the Spirit of God is in us. *Compare Romans 6:1-16, 17-23, read Romans, chapters 7 and 8*

[Romans 6:14-18 ESV] 14 For sin will have no dominion over you, since you are not under law but under grace. 15 What then? Are we to sin because we are not under law but under grace? By no means! 16 Do you not know that if you present yourselves to anyone as obedient slaves, you are slaves of the one whom you obey, either of sin, which leads to death, or of obedience, which leads to righteousness? 17 But thanks be to God, that you who were once slaves of sin have become obedient from the heart to the standard of teaching to which you were committed, 18 and, having been set free from sin, have become slaves of righteousness.

You Are Worthy

Lyrics and Melody by **Faye A. Cross~ Inspired by Holy Spirit; Written: 11/27/2015** *Copyright 2015-2017 © All rights reserved*

I found there's freedom -There's freedom from the law *(background)* **You are worthy** But I'm captive in my heart- to the law of love I'm drawn **You are worthy** I no longer live - to satisfy my sinful flesh **You are worthy** I'm captive to you Jesus - to your righteousness **You are worthy** And it's your heart that makes me feel and know that I am blessed **You are worthy**

Chorus:

You are worthy, You are worthy You are worthy Jesus - repeat Great and marvelous are thy ways Lord God Almighty - Just and true are thy ways, thou King of saints **(repeat)**

Chorus/Bridge:

Awesome God Mighty God Prince of Peace Wonderful Counselor Eternal Father - Alpha Omega Righteous Ruler Majestic One Holy One King of Kings Lord of Lords My Savior Redeemer...I found there's freedom I'm grateful for this place I found... **You are worthy** With boldness I'm before you now though with a humble heart **You are worthy** I found the secret place -- where love abounds and I feel safe **You are worthy**

It's this place - where glory shines upon your lovely face **You are worthy** I see grace, where mercy lives, the place where sinners are saved **You are worthy**

Chorus:

You are worthy, You are worthy You are worthy, Jesus -**repeat** Great and marvelous are thy ways Lord God Almighty - Just and true are thy ways, thou King of saints **(repeat)**

December 2015

12/5/2015 THE MAKING OF "GLORY ARISES"

(Wedding Song Waltz)

I give God thanks and ALL the praise, glory and honor for his great name, for he is worthy. May I share with you some manna I found in this song the Lord has given me to share with you. You've already read how the song **"Lamb of God (Cross and Calvary)"** came about. Also you know about the song, **"Lay Him Down"** was birthed out of **"Lamb of God"**. Well, this is another song that was born out of **"Lamb of God"**. It's called **"Glory Arises (Wedding Song Waltz)**.

I haven't recorded this song yet. I know when I do it will be something extra special. I have the melody which is the melody of **"Lamb of God"**. It's just a matter of time when the Holy Spirit will help me to bring it all together. Now what the Lord helped me to see in regards to this song, it is a prophetic picture of the **LAMB** as the **KING of KINGS** and **LORD of LORDS, the KING OF GLORY, THE MIGHTY GOD and EVERLASTING FATHER** over all the earth. John wrote it down as he saw it too in Revelations. So he not only showed me that but also told me there are lyrics to the song. He gave me the lyrics today. He continued showing me that the music I played was with the strings voice on the keyboard and he said that the strings stay but the main voice of this song is the

HARP which is mentioned in Rev 14:2. So I'm thinking, OK Lord. The 144,000 will have this song mastered by the time you come to stand on Mt Zion.

God will bring peace and harmony and bless all of his creation when Jesus returns in the second coming. All creation groans and sighs awaiting this day. When he stands on the hill, Mount Zion as I hear the angels singing in the background as well as hallelujah, this he will do in his appointed time. The **GLORY ARISES** on the day of **NEW BEGINNINGS. GLORY TO GOD!**

Below are the lyrics that I am sure will bless you as you relate to their meaning. Glory to God!

Glory Arises aka The Wedding Song Waltz

Lyrics and melody by **Faye A. Cross**

Inspired by the Holy Spirit

Based on Rev 14: 1-5, Zech 14: 4, 7-9, Isa 9:6, Rev 3:14

Verse 1

Yah Almighty Begins to reign as his Glory Arises Bless His Holy name; Yah bless the people in the land the Almighty Comes w/ power He stands; Yah brings a unique day to begin Amen, Messiah the living Word, will never rescind

Chorus:

Hallelujah 8 X

Standing on a hill, Standing on a mount

Standing on the earth there's no more curse

Yah Almighty, Believe in Him... His Glory Arises Bringing end to sin; Standing on a hill , standing on a mount HalleluYah, halleluYah; His banner flag raised over all the earth... signaling peace reverse the curse

Chorus:

HalleluYah 8 X

Standing on a hill, Standing on a mount

Standing on the earth there's no more curse

Bridge:

He comes in the Father's name, his kingdom we proclaim

He came, he died for you and I

We have new life in him death swallowed up with sin

He saves our life from sin and strife

Gifts brought from near and far bearing his name

He stands with power in the judgment hour

Chorus:

Hallelujah 8 X

Standing on a hill, Standing on a mount

Standing on the earth there's no more curse

12/16/2015 Vibrant rainbow on my door

On December 16, 2015 on a Wednesday afternoon the most beautiful rainbow colors appeared on my living room door leading to the room I had been recording in earlier in the day. I was relaxing on the couch in the living room when I noticed the rainbow colors on the door.

It seemed to appear out of nowhere, for I was not expecting it. I've been living in this apartment since 2009 and never have any rainbow colors appeared on my door. It was extremely bright and vibrant, most beautiful, so I immediately got my camera and video taped the rainbow colors. Glory to God! It had been around 2 months to the day since when the Lord blessed me with the **flashing rainbow** colored **mouth light** at the church talent show where I sang **"Yeshua's Wedding Day"**. *See Journal 10/16/2015 for details.*

One day in 2013 I was singing to the Lord while recording and while I'm singing directly to the Lord praising him, a brilliant array of rainbow colors came shooting through the window and hit the paper I had in my hand. It was all recorded on video. I still have that video but I'm not able to get it off of my old laptop computer. I knew at that precise moment the Lord wanted to give me a direct signal from heaven's throne room how pleased he was with my praise and worship in the song. He is so kind and loving towards us.

So far, the Lord has blessed me with **four rainbows** connected to my songs of praise and worship to him. You've heard about the first three so far. I can't wait to tell you later about the fourth one. All this talk about rainbows reminds me of what John saw in heaven when he was called up. He recorded what he saw at **Revelation 4:2-3**, KJV

*"And immediately, I was in the spirit: and, behold, **a throne was set in heaven**, **and one sat on the throne**. And he that sat was to look upon like a jasper and a sardine stone: **and there was a rainbow round about the throne, in sight like unto an emerald.**"*

January 2016

The Making of "Israel Lift Up Thine Eyes"

It all started with me singing in the Spirit. Something I had never done before was record myself singing in the Spirit as I did this day. As I listened to the playback I really liked the melody which sounded beautiful to me. I had never heard this melody before and I started praying asking God what I was saying. I started hearing Israel over and over initially and the other lyrics just flowed as I was writing them down. I love it when the Holy Spirit gives me the melody and words altogether. There was no struggle and not many rewrites. One of my sisters told me she really loves this song. I have to admit it is one of my favorites of all the songs the Lord has given me. It has been one of the hardest songs to record as well.

I've received much opposition from the enemy when it comes to recording this song. My voice cracks, squeaks and breaks making me sound off key and strained almost every time I try to record it. I've changed the lyrics over and over, in particular the first verse. What I heard initially I kept going back to change it, for some odd reason it just did not set well with my spirit. This is what the first verse was before I changed it recently for about the tenth time going back and forth.

Where once stood my Holy Place, lies darkness and abomination...

I kept changing this first line because in my heart I kept thinking what if the DOTR is not in the place where God's Holy Place was, what if they are mistaken. And if that is the case, then I would be calling what is still HOLY not holy. I only know one thing, IF the DOTR is actually in the place where the Lord's Holy of Holies was, then that statement **STANDS TRUE.** But right now the experts question the veracity of the supposed exact location of the Holy of Holies. Fear set in I must admit. I'm not perfect. Someday I will understand it all.

Compare Isaiah 62:1-12, 65:17-25

Israel Lift Up Thine Eyes

Melody and Lyrics by **Faye A. Cross and Holy Spirit** ~ Written: 01/16/2016 All rights reserved Copyright 2016 © (BMI) Lyrics updated 7/4/2017 **Based on:** Isaiah 60:1-4, 1Peter 2:9, Matthew 24:15, Zechariah 2:8, Hebrews 10:22, Gal 4:25-26 and Rev 19:6

Israel, lift up thine eyes, for you I sent my Son to die

Israel, arise and shine, you are the apple of my eye

Main Verse
Inside your heart, now my Holy Place, lies the Light of Salvation

Unashamed you carry my name as a light before the nations

My Royal Priesthood, my Holy Nation, you are a Chosen Generation, My love for you is not in question, to you Israel, I make this declaration

Chorus:
Israel, lift up thine eyes, for you I sent my Son to die; **JESUS Christ** is HIS great name, sing Hallelu**Yah** lift your voice and say; **Israel,** arise and shine, you are the apple of my eye; Jerusalem, your light has come Oh Zion don't you see your Holy One

Bridge:
Jerusalem above will set you free Jerusalem above will set you free; Israel, Israel, O' Israel

Main Verse
In many hearts, now my Holy Place lies the Rock of ALL ages

Unafraid you've carried my name as a light throughout the ages

My Holy Nation, special possession, you are a Chosen Generation; My love for you is not in question, to you today, I make this declaration

2nd Chorus
Israel, your king is here, to every heart He calls to draw you near; **Yeshua** (**JESUS**) is HIS name, the ONLY name you need to be saved; **Israel,** arise and shine, sons and daughters come to feast and dine; Drink new wine, taste liberty! Sweet as honey, taste your **Jubilee**

1st Bridge:
Jerusalem above will set you free Jerusalem above will set you free; Israel, Israel, O' Israel

2nd Bridge:
Israel, Oh Israel lift up your eyes, for you I sent my son to die

Look up and see what you can be this is the year of your Jubilee; Look up and see Jerusalem above, she will set you free, how good is liberty; It's Oh so sweet, sweet as honey, sweet as honey I'm your Jubilee **Oh** Israel, Israel, you have my heart, forever together, we'll never part; Arise and shine, arise and shine, you'll always be the apple of my eye; You will always be, a part of ME, a part of me for all eternity; Lift up thine eyes, arise and shine, You are the apple of my eye

March 2016

New Keyboard

The Lord answered my prayer for a new keyboard that had extra voices on it and just a better overall quality. The keyboard was like new with top of the line accessories. A young lady said she never developed an interest in learning to play it. I thought oh yes, that's because it was meant for me. Glory to God!

April 2016

4/2/2016 La Boda (The Wedding)

La Boda (The Wedding) is the next to last song the Lord has given me for **"DWTK CD"**. It is the pinnacle, climax and highlight of this **C**hrist **D**irected **CD** project. It has a sound quality and lyrical richness that resonates deep within my heart and soul. When I listen to it I imagine myself in heaven during the wedding feast of the Lamb. I can't wait to see the final restoration of all things culminating with a new heavens and new earth.

More Equipment Challenges Met by God

I don't know how many times I've said I never know when the Holy Spirit is going to lead me in creating a new song. When I get on the keyboard I am usually practicing one of the songs we've already written together but I love it when He moves me to try something new. It was on Saturday, April 2, 2016 that I was moved to try out some new voices on my new keyboard I bought last month. I'd been looking for a new keyboard for some months with no success. I was looking on craigslist, amazon.com, ebay, and other online businesses that sell musical instruments. The prices were always out of my range and most private sellers are not as flexible as I had hoped they would be or maybe I'm just not a good negotiator. I had a perfectly good keyboard that worked just fine and then one day the plug just stopped working. So I would have to use batteries that would only last a day or two at the most. Imagine the money I would have to spend just to practice everyday which I was doing around this time.

I know inexpensive batteries may not last that long but even so cheap batteries should last at least 3-4 or more days I would think. But I was buying the most expensive Duracell batteries and they wouldn't last more than 2 days. Pretty much all of my equipment stopped working, my laptop and desktop computers along with my printer. I knew what was happening.

I prayed and my friends prayed that God would make a way for me to get equipment that would work. **Answered prayer:** So here I was in need of a new keyboard that I could plug in so I wouldn't have to use batteries and of course he came through. The Lord didn't stop with the keyboard. He must have gotten tired of me asking and begging for help. He came through in every area, fixing the printer and computer. I took my computer to a repair shop where the gentleman not only fixed the problem but gave me extra ram for free and a new operating system for half the regular price. God's favor and grace were poured out on me. To God be the glory. So getting back to Saturday, I started tinkering around with some of the new voices I got with this new keyboard that I didn't have on the other keyboard. Voices are different instrument sounds arranger keyboards come equipped with. For instance, in addition to the normal piano sounds, you can play on the same keyboard other instrument voices like electric pianos, organs, violins, cellos, harps, flutes, guitars, trumpets, saxophones and orchestral strings.

Testing the New Keyboard

The first new voice I decided to test was the saxophone voice. My other keyboard had all the same voices including a saxophone voice but this new keyboard had some additional voice patterns or versions of the saxophone that sounded different. I never tried using the saxophone on the other keyboard but now I am.

I found a nice beat and started playing the keyboard. I let the Lord lead me in playing whatever chords he wanted. I got my first keyboard in June 2015 so I had only been experimenting with the keyboard at this time for about 10 months. It so happens my favorite chords, **C Major 7** and **F Major 7** are used a lot in jazz music.

I have come to the conclusion through my musical journey with the Lord that He **LOVES JAZZ** music. You may not believe me in saying that if you don't have a personal taste for jazz music. I find jazz relaxing because it's easy listening music, but we will all certainly find out when we get to heaven for sure. We certainly can't put the Lord in a box but some of us do. He created music with all the chords and notes we have and they are **ALL from HIM**, not the enemy.

Underneath the Surface

While listening to the instrumental playback recording I kept hearing the word **"BODA"**. That's Spanish for **"WEDDING"**. I also heard very distinctly **"Vencedores"** which is Spanish for **"Overcomers' ' and "se venceras la vida"** which means "will overcome or conquer life" . Right away I knew the name of the song should be **La Boda (The Wedding).** The Lord led me to play it again the next day and it sounded like He was refining the melody for me. As I played back the recording I heard distinctly the word **"Hosanna"**. Two days later on April 4th I started writing the lyrics in both English and Spanish.

The wedding day is soon to come. All the signs are pointing in that direction. The Lord does not want to lose any that belong to him. He died for the whole world.

It will happen in His own **perfect** timing with the **full number of Gentiles** and the **full number of 144,000** made up of the twelve tribes of Israel which together makes **ONE** new man **complete** in God. HalleluYAH!!! Compare *Rev 7:4-8 Gal 3:8 Gen 18:18 and Rom 2:29*

[Romans 11:25 NIV] 25 I do not want you to be ignorant of this mystery, brothers and sisters, so that you may not be conceited: Israel has experienced a hardening in part until the full number of the Gentiles has come in...

Again I found myself dancing with the Lord in my heart of hearts the night I composed **La Boda** as I listened to it over and over again. The Lord created music for all of us to enjoy. The enemy has contaminated much of the music today as He has with lots of things in this world. But that doesn't have to stop us from enjoying pure hearted wholesome music.

*[1 John 2:14 NASB] 14 I have written to you, ... and the **word of God abides in you** and you have **overcome** the evil one*

PROPHETIC SONG ~ INSPIRED BY THE HOLY SPIRIT

Based on: **Psalm 45:3, 9, 11 and Revelation 19:7, Acts 3:21, Rev 3:21, Ezek 43:2**

La Boda (The Wedding) © *Melody/ lyrics by* **Faye A. Cross** *Melody composed: 2 April 2016 English and Spanish lyrics written: 4 April 2016 Copyright 2016 © All rights reserved (BMI)*

Verse 1: Overcomers you made it through, through the fire your faith was proved; Jesus sees his beauty in you Majestic King, Mighty & BOLD, the bride's made ready, BEHOLD to rule with you on heaven's throne

Chorus: La Boda! The day will come, the wedding of the Lamb will come soon some day! Hosanna! Hosanna in the highest! The day will come, when all creation will celebrate the restoration of all things made new, just for me and you! Morning stars, celestial bouquets, adorn the sky AND Milky Way, HOLY is this wedding day, this moment in time La Boda! The day will come, the wedding of the Lamb will come soon, we pray! Hosanna! Hosanna in the highest!

Bridge: There's no love deeper or higher than YOURS! Let all creation praise you Jesus forevermore! I'll always love and honor you as my Lord to praise your name forever is my prize reward

Music interlude (2 bars)

Verse 2: Rushing waters, hear them roar, peals of thunder ROLLing forth; the sound of His COMING echoes LOVE, Chords of LOVE in our hearts are stored, with melodies never heard before, now OUR hearts ARE ALL in ONE accord!

Chorus: La Boda! The day will come, the wedding of the Lamb will come soon, we pray! Hosanna! Hosanna in the highest! The day will come, when every nation will rise to love and reconciliation. Love is the key for true peace and harmony! There'll be rainbows high in the sky ordained by YAHWEH THE MOST HIGH, HOLY is this wedding day, and moment in time; La Boda! Hosanna Princess bride and Messiah You're the Father's heart desire! La Boda! Hosanna Behold the Lion of Judah It must be his wedding day! **Bridge:** There's no love deeper or higher than YOURS! Let all creation praise you Jesus forevermore! I'll always love and honor you as my Lord to praise your name forever is my prize reward

Music interlude (2 bars)

Chorus: La Boda! The day will come, the wedding of the Lamb will come soon, we pray! Hosanna! Hosanna in the highest! The day will come, when every nation will celebrate the coronation Of Jesus crowned ruler and king! Morning stars, celestial bouquets, adorn the sky AND Milky Way, HOLY is this wedding day, this moment in time La Boda! The day will come, the wedding of the Lamb will come soon, we pray! Hosanna! Hosanna in the highest!

La Boda (The Wedding) versión Española ©

Melody and lyrics by **Faye A. Cross** *Melody composed: 2 April 2016 English and Spanish lyrics written: 4 April 2016 Copyright 2016 © All rights reserved (BMI)*

Versículo 1: Vencedores lo hiciste a través, a través del fuego tu fe fue probada; Jesús ve su belleza dentro de ti Rey majestuoso, eres fuerte y audaz, las novias preparadas, BEHOLD para gobernar contigo en el trono del cielo

Estribillo: La Boda! ¡El día vendrá, la boda del cordero vendrá pronto algún día! Hosanna ¡Hosanna en lo más alto! ¡El día vendrá, cuando toda la creación celebrará la restauración de todas las cosas hechas nuevas, sólo para mí y para ti! Estrellas de la mañana, ramos celestiales, adornan el cielo Y la Vía Láctea, SANTO es este día de la boda, este momento La Boda! ¡El día vendrá, la boda del cordero vendrá pronto que oramos! Hosanna ¡Hosanna en lo más alto!
Puente: No hay amor más profundo o más alto que el SUYO! ¡Deja que toda la creación te alabe a Jesús para siempre! Siempre te amaré y te honraré como mi Señor Am para alabar tu nombre para siempre es mi premio recompensa Intermedio de música **(2 barras)**

Versículo 2: Aguas que corren, los oyen rugir, gritos de trueno ROLLING adelante; el sonido de sus ecos venidos AMOR, Los acordes del AMOR en nuestros corazones se almacenan, con las melodías nunca antes oídas, ahora

¡NUESTROS corazones ESTÁN TODOS en UN acuerdo!

Estribillo: La Boda! ¡El día vendrá, la boda del cordero vendrá pronto que oramos! Hosanna ¡Hosanna en lo más alto! El día vendrá, cuando cada nación se levante para el amor y la reconciliación El amor es la clave para la verdadera paz y armonía! Habrá arco iris arriba en el cielo ordenado por YAHWEH EL MÁS ALTO, SANTO es este día de la boda, y momento en el tiempo; La Boda! Hosanna Princesa novia y Mesías ¡Eres el deseo del corazón del Padre! La Boda! Hosanna Behold el león de Judah ¡Debe ser su día de la boda. **Puente:** No hay amor más profundo o más alto que el SUYO! ¡Deja que toda la creación te alabe a Jesús para siempre! Siempre te amaré y te honraré como mi Señor Am para alabar tu nombre para siempre es mi premio recompensa Intermedio de música **(2 barras)**

Verso 3: corriendo aguas, oirlos rugir, a lo largo de la orilla arenosa; se oyen pájaros cantando dulces acordes melódicos, Se restauran los acordes de AMOR en nuestros corazones, con melodías nunca antes escuchadas, ¡ ahora nuestros corazones ESTÁN UNO! **Repeat Estribillo:**

4/22/2016 La Boda (Amazing Grace) Instrumental

This has been a long time favorite hymn of many people over the years. I interweaved this amazing hymn with the melody of La Boda creating a new instrumental song for the many grateful hearts of Jesus, our true Amazing Grace. It's short but sweet.

June 2016

6/4/2016 WALKING WITH JESUS

(Along the River of Life)

This is one of my favorite songs because it comes from **La Boda**, an instrumental song that has such a profound meaning behind the chords. No matter which instrument voice on the keyboard I play the melody of **La Boda**, it's a winner. In **"Walking with Jesus"** I am playing the flute voice on my keyboard for the same melody of **La Boda**. It's a sure winner. When I listen to it I always imagine I'm walking along the river of life in heaven with my Lord and Savior, Jesus. What are we talking about? I can't tell you. Why, because I don't know yet. :) Whatever it is I know one thing for sure, he's making me laugh. Do you ever imagine what it will be like in heaven? Do you meditate on the fact that we will be walking on the streets of **GOLD one day soon?** We will be blessed! He will literally wipe away every tear from our eyes.

[Rev 21:3-4 NIV] 3 And I heard a loud voice from the throne saying, "Look! God's dwelling place is now among the people, and he will dwell with them. They will be his people, and God himself will be with them and be their God. 4 'He will wipe every tear from their eyes. There will be no more death' or mourning or crying or pain, for the old order of things has passed away."

[Isaiah 65:17 NIV] 17 "See, I will create new heavens and a new earth. The former things will not be remembered, nor will they come to mind.

6/27/2016 Yahweh That's His Name

On Monday evening I was just playing around on the keyboard playing some of the songs I had recently written like La Boda. As I turned on the video camera to record I began singing to the melody coming forth. The song turned out to be a beautiful song of me expressing my love for my heavenly Father Yahweh. Some call him only by the English name **Jehovah** which I do at times. One of my favorite songs to sing is **"Because of Who You Are"**, a popular song by Vicki Yohe. But I do like the Hebrew name **Yahweh** as well. I think the Hebrew language has a beautiful sound to it. I love to speak in different languages. In the song which was totally spontaneous, I speak of **Yahweh** as being the **El Shaddai**.

I've known God to be many things to me, not just a loving father but the comfort of a mother, a brother, sister, doctor, lawyer, friend, husband, etc., etc. Many times we find the Lord in people he put in our lives. As a woman in Christ I can be the mother or a sister to someone the Lord leads me to.

You perhaps a man in Christ can be a father or a brother to whomever the Lord has drawn you to. **El Shaddai** is not a name I normally use or have ever really thought about or given any consideration to in the past. Therefore, I know for a fact the Holy Spirit put that name in my mind as I was singing. He was leading me all the way. So, I was led to look up some information on **El Shaddai** because though I had heard the name before I didn't know exactly what it meant.

In my research I discovered that **El Shaddai** was the name God was known by **BEFORE** he was known by his personal name **"YHWH"** pronounced as **Yahweh** in Hebrew and **Jehovah** in English. **El Shaddai** means **"Mighty God"**. Yes, isn't that something, we serve a Mighty God but it means so much more. [7]I found this definition of **El Shaddai** on the website www.parentcompany.com interesting.

[7]*El-Shaddai, means **God Almighty**. El points to the power of God Himself. **Shaddai**, seems to be derived from another word **meaning breast**, which implies that Shaddai signifies one who **nourishes, supplies,** and **satisfies**. It is God as El who helps, but it is God as Shaddai **who abundantly blesses with all manner of blessings**."*

God created man in his image, both **MALE and FEMALE** he made them. I know this is controversial in some ways so I won't say anything more. I'm not saying Jesus is a woman or that God is a woman. Please don't misunderstand me.

I'm saying that in God are the qualities that he put inside of the woman, which are to nurture and care for others which is LOVE in action. There are many supporting scriptures to back that statement. I will list only a few of them but you may go to the direct article on the above referenced website, the link is provided in the reference section at the end of the book or you may google El Shaddai to get more information.

It blessed my soul to read this about El Shaddai, the God of Abraham, Isaac and Jacob. This was the Holy Spirit leading me in coming to know more about who God is. He is COMPLETE in all of his children, both MALE and FEMALE. I believe this is why in Christ there is neither male nor female because we are ALL ONE in encompassing him. God encompasses all the qualities we see in man created in his image, demonstrated in LOVE. He is the essence or the total embodiment of LOVE. El Shaddai is merely the two sides of God which encompass his MIGHT as it literally means MIGHTY GOD. It is the dominant male character we see of a Father's protection and guidance factor, so may we recognize and acknowledge that in Him. Also, it reminds us of his nurturing compassionate side He demonstrates in love. I lost my mother in 1974 so I was happy to learn about this side of God's character. Now I could appreciate the comfort that the Holy Spirit brings in His holy presence.

Yahweh, that's his name

Lyrics/ melody by **Faye A. Cross** *Inspired by the Holy Spirit Written: 6/27/16 All rights reserved Copyright © 2016 (BMI)*

[Psalm 29:2] "**Ascribe to Yahweh the glory due His name**; *worship in the splendor of His Holiness*" **HCSB [Psalm 92:1-2, 4-5, 8 NIV]** *1 A psalm. A song. For the Sabbath day. It is good to praise the LORD and make* **music to your name, O Most High**, *2 proclaiming your love in the morning and your faithfulness at night, ... 4 For you make me glad by your deeds, LORD; I sing for joy at what your hands have done. 5 How great are your works, LORD, how profound your thoughts! ... 8 But you, LORD, are forever exalted.*

Intro:

Yahweh, Yahweh, that's his name; I would like to sing his name Yahweh, Yahweh, Yahweh, that's his name; He's so perfect and true in every way Yahweh, And I just want to sing this song to you today pause. La da da ta da la da da ta da da da da yeh repeat

Verse 1

I don't know what I'm gonna say; I just gonna speak from my heart; This song was not planned in any way, not any part

But I just keep hearing in my heart Yahweh, I keep hearing in my heart Yahweh Yahweh today, He is beautiful to me..... you see , I love everything about my God, Yahweh; He created me, He formed me in my mother's wound,He planned out my days in every way yes He did Yahweh, Whatever He says to me He fulfills, He is a God that cannot lie, cheat or steal; He's not like man, imperfect in his ways.... cause He's the Ancient of days; He's perfection in every way...El Shaddai, the Most High, Yahweh..El Shaddai, the Most High Yahweh....

Bridge:

I'm gonna give Him all the praise, gonna give Him all the praise that I can do. I'm gonna worship you with all my heart that's all I want to do, in this song, that I sing for you Yahweh

Chorus 2:

Your name's so beautiful I just wanna say Yahweh, Yahweh

I wake up everyday knowing that I'm loved by Yahweh Yahweh, Yahweh, Yahweh, Yahweh, Yahweh, Yahweh, Yahweh Yahweh Yahweh Yahweh...Yahweh Yahweh Yahweh Yah Yah Yahweh Yahweh ...that's all I want to say is Yahweh, I want to praise you today I want to praise you with this song Yahweh today..Ancient of days, El Shaddai, the Most High

Thank you Jesus for revealing the Father to me; for he's no longer, thanks to you a mystery; you are the mystery hidden in God for centuries; And now today we can say we really know you, Yahweh. You're the essence of love, perfect in every way Yahweh...Jesus the Rock strong and mighty You are GRACE, his favor and mercy, Father, Holy Spirit and Son, through you His heart I've won; You're the essence of love perfect in every way, Yahweh, Yahweh you're the essence of love perfect in every way...Jesus, thank you Jesus, (repeat)

Through you the open door, I've found He's everything and more ...You're the essence of love perfect in every way, Yahweh, Yahweh you're the essence of love perfect in every way... *Isaiah 60:15-16, Isaiah 66:10-13, and Rev 16:7, 14*

July 2016

7/12/2016 The Answer To A Special Prayer

This was a special month for several reasons. For the most part it was a month full of severe spiritual warfare yet a month I saw the awe inspiring **GLORY** of God. I wrote a prayer on **July 12, 2016** that I posted on my bedroom wall and later my blog website, the Lord's ministry Morning Manna with Love. One of the things I wrote down and prayed was for **Father Yahweh (Jehovah)** to show me his **GLORY.** I addressed **Jesus (Yeshua)** specifically to **reveal the Father** to me as he promised he would reveal the Father to us at Luke 10:22. *See below*

[Luke 10:22 NIV] 22 "All things have been committed to me by my Father. No one knows who the Son is except the Father, and **no one knows who the Father is except** the Son and **those to whom the Son chooses to reveal him**."

I kid you not, the very next day, **7/13/2016** started out like a normal day though it was a little overcast. Around 5:30-6:00 pm, it started to lightly rain and as I looked out my bedroom window I noticed the biggest rainbow I'd ever seen in my life. I started shouting and praising the Lord. I quickly put on a jacket and rushed to go outside. As I went to the elevator I saw two of my neighbors sitting on a nearby bench and I told them I was in a hurry to get outside to take a picture.

God had sent this glorious rainbow for me to see. I had been singing about His rainbow over and over for the past two months, a song I wrote titled **LaBoda (The Wedding)**. One line in the chorus says: *"Rainbows set high in the sky, ordained by Yahweh, the Most High".* I was so excited because I just knew in my heart that this was God answering my prayer. I had prayed the day before asking Jesus to show me the Father's glory. It didn't occur to me until later about the rainbow being his **GLORY.** *Genesis 9:13-14, 16*

[Gen 9:13-14, 16 KJV] 13 I do set my bow in the cloud, and it shall be for a token of a covenant between me and the earth. 14 And it shall come to pass, when I bring a cloud over the earth, that the bow shall be seen in the cloud: ... 16 And the bow shall be in the cloud; and I will look upon it, that I may remember the everlasting covenant between God and every living creature of all flesh that [is] upon the earth.

As I'm writing this now, I realize the Lord had been showing me HIS glory all along as I was dancing with the King. It didn't occur till now that He was showing me the glory in gradual stages as it turned out to be. He showed me a small glimpse of glory the first time in 2011. I was videotaping myself singing a song I had written at the time. It was cloudy as I sat by the window with the blinds slightly opened. I began singing the first verse and when I got to the chorus singing praises to the Lord, suddenly the clouds opened up as the sun shined brightly. On the playback I could see the brilliance of the sun shining through the blinds which created this beautiful iridescent rainbow effect on the lyrics sheet I was holding.

Unfortunately I haven't been able to recover that video from the laptop it was saved on. But that's okay because I can still see it in my mind's eye. It was just a tiny peek by comparison of today's full rainbow yet it was glorious and an unforgettable moment. All the JOY I felt at the time has come back flooding my memory as I recall watching that video over and over just to see the beautiful rainbow effect on the paper as I praised the Lord. The next time that He showed me His **GLORY** was at a church function in October 2015 where I sang Yeshua's Wedding day acapella, another song Holy Spirit inspired me to write. At the church fundraiser event I won a **RAINBOW** mouth light, one of the few door prizes given out that night. You may now recall me telling you about this incident earlier. I got a good chuckle out of that appreciating the Lord's sense of humor and kindness. I give the Most High all the GLORY!

How awesome is the Lord! A few months later the Lord showed me another representation of His glory shining rainbow colors on the door as I was relaxing on the couch. The majestic splendor of the Lord caught me by surprise again. The colors were extremely vibrant. It was at least 12 inches in width, maybe 4 or five inches in height. Today I went outside in the rain to make a video of the rainbow. This would be the fourth time God would show me His glory. Amazing! What a magnificent sight it was to behold!

It appeared unimaginably huge within a close range of view, so close it felt like I could reach out and touch it. I've seen rainbow pics and videos where most appear to be in the far off distance. I had seen a rainbow in the sky only once before in all my life back in the sixties. This made the rainbow that much more special because it's not something you see everyday. I know my neighbors thought I was going bonkers over seeing a rainbow. They looked at me strangely as I rushed outside, shouting and praising God. I wasn't putting on a show for anyone. I was genuinely excited because I **KNEW** without a doubt this was a **DIRECT** answer to my prayer request to see God's glory.

Can you understand how enormous this would boost my faith in the Lord as I had been learning to dance this dance of faith and grace with him? You have read of my trials I had thus far gone through just to get to this point in my calling and walk with God. One neighbor did follow me outside and she's on the video speaking about the rainbow being a sign that God would never destroy the world again with water. I was so happy that Ms Lula joined me in praising the Lord. I wasn't surprised at all because I knew she loves the Lord immensely and loves to talk about Him all the time every chance she gets. Thank you Lord for such a beautiful experience to share. Glory to God Most High!!!

STILL DANCING WITH MY KING

Thanks for sticking with me this far. In my dance, I discovered His plans for me were more than I could ever dream of. Amazingly, He showed me my life in various stages through dreams of things I would go through for the kingdom's sake. I've seen most come true, so I'm confident that everything will come to pass. Some of my journal entries left me wondering whether all of my experiences were of the Holy Spirit or was it a deceiving spirit. I concluded not all was of the Holy Spirit, yet, I wanted to share everything, good, bad and ugly. I was going through baby steps. Always test the spirit.

My timeline ends in the year of 2016, although much has happened since then, as you can imagine. Hopefully I've grown some and continue to progress in Him. I continued to keep my journal pretty regularly up until around the end of 2018. Maybe if it's the Lord's will there may be a second volume coming. It's taken more years than expected to write part one. Primarily, fear of exposing myself with the public was my biggest fear. So, yes I got chicken even though I had made a promise to God that I would be as open and transparent as possible, especially when I could possibly help someone in similar circumstances. For a long time the manuscript lay dormant. Sometimes we begin doing other things for the Lord that's of our own doing. If the timing is wrong, we're out of line.

Lessons Learned For A Time Such As This

Having said that, life goes on and we get busy with our lives. Sometimes working for the Lord is done at the expense of not spending enough quality time with Him in bible study and one on one worship time. We simply overwork ourselves feeling too tired to spend time with the Lord. For another it may be working to support their family, hobbies or other pursuits that are not wrong in themselves but keep us from spending enough quality time with Him. In any case, we can become off balance not walking in the complete will of God.

*[**Matthew 6:33 KJV**] 33 But seek ye first the kingdom of God, and his righteousness; and all these things shall be added unto you.*

As I dance with the King of Kings, he continually unveils himself to me revealing who He is and what He requires of me. The church as a whole, myself included, has failed somewhat miserably in keeping God's will first. In 2020, He got everyone's attention with the coronavirus. I'm not saying He caused the virus but many have concluded, myself included, that it was permitted by Him for a specific purpose. The reason was to get us to stop chasing after our own selfish pursuits which are nothing but vanity, chasing after the wind.

How many of us learned that ministry can become an idol. Anything keeping us out of God's will can become an idol. Some of us may have thought we were in the will of God but were not. Our intentions were good but priorities were out of place.

I'm a work in progress trying to find my balance in this matter. *Matthew 6:33* Putting the kingdom first is crucial but the KING of that kingdom is above all things. The church is called to be of one mind and heart in this regard. I've also learned to see the hidden beauty in the storms. One special blessing I received in my dance is how Jesus redirected me back to my first love, my love for the Father which I somewhat alluded to earlier. Knowing the Father is in Jesus, I talked to Jesus about the Father asking him to reveal more of the Father to me. My heart was in need of a father's love.

He's revealed to me extraordinary things about the Father and what He and the Father's will were for me. *Compare Luke 10:21-22 and John 16:23-25* The Father filled me with His Spirit coming to me when I called upon His name late in the middle of the night. He would later give me songs that I still love singing today, one particular where I can lift up His name **Yahweh** in praise and worship. Just a few more lessons I've learned to appreciate. This is where the Lord has led me to today, in 2023. Now I can see how all the projects I'd been working on serve a purpose in getting me to the point of writing and finishing **"My Dance with the King of Kings"**. I always knew He wanted to speak through me a message for a time such as this for the bride church, but not at the expense of neglecting my first love. The day of the Lord's return draws nearer and those songs you saw in my journal timeline were written for today though I wrote them years ago.

Now is the time to get our focus and attention on the things of heaven because the day of the Lord draws nearer each day. Some may say Babylon is falling. Time is ticking away for this world as we know it today. The bride must be ready. She makes herself ready by being separate from this world which has a hold on most people of the world without their notice, care or objection. Are you getting yourself ready for the coming of the Lord? Are you prepared, knowing He'll come when we least expect? How do you know if you're in the world but not **OF** the world? *John 17:15-16*

The "ME" Generation

We are the generation labeled as the **ME generation.** We live in a world that shouts everyday everything's all about "**ME**". The words **selfie**, **YouTube** and **I-phone** have taken on profound significance in describing the world's selfish, self absorbed culture of this **ME** generation. Even the world knows time is tick-tocking away as they fancy social media's TikTok. We're all susceptible to getting caught up in this web of deception. **Me, me, me** is the global mantra call, echoing across planet earth. It's taken effect upon persons of every age group, race, economical status or religion. [5] I made a list of words beginning with the letters, **"M" and "E",** that I felt precisely characterizes this **"ME" generation..**

[8] W. E. Vines 2005 for scriptural references.

Marriage: increase of divorce 2 Timothy 3:1-5

Masturbation: pornography, immorality 1 Corinthians 6:9

Murder: manslayer, hatred; violence Gen 6:13, 2 Timothy 3:3

Money: mammon, riches, greed, corruption Luke 6:9,11,13

Mythology: folklore, wive's tales, myths, lies 1 Timothy 4:6-7

Mask: disguise true character Mark 7:6, Matthew 24:51

Mark: distinctive character mark of the beast Revelation 14:9-10

Materialistic: value material things over spiritual Revelation 3:17

Mischievous: harmful behavior, evil, injurious Luke 11:29

Mistrust: lack of confidence, reject truth 1 Peter 2:7

Endtime (last days) people proud, arrogant 2 Timothy 3:1-5

Earthy: carnal, governed by human nature/lust 1 Peter 2:11

Evil-doers: wicked, hates the light John 3:20

Error: forsaking the right way; no morals Jude 11

Enslaved: become a slave; e.g. (too much wine) Titus 2:3

Entangled: held in a yoke of bondage 2 Peter 2:20

Enemy: opposed to God; an adversary Nahum 1:2

Empty: hollow, vain, the absence of quality Acts 4:25

Enticements: lured by bait, lust, seducement 2 Peter 2:14

Eye-service: pretentious, hypocritical, insincere Colossians 3:22

Effeminate: male lewdness, sins of the flesh 1 Corinthians 6:9

Envy: jealousy and strife; confusion James 3:16

Egypt: symbol of bondage, carnality, the world Numbers 14:2

Entertainment:lovers of pleasure rather than God 2 Timothy 3:4

The Endtime Esau Generation

The bible describes in precise terms what the world would look like in the last days at *2 Timothy 3:1-5* Critical times are what we're dealing with. *Matthew 24:37-39* Most notably, the **ME-generation** is flawed with the markings of a familiar person found in the Old Testament named **ESAU**. Esau was the older twin brother of **JACOB,** sons of Isaac and Rebekah. Esau sold his birthright blessing to Jacob for a bowl of red stew. What can we learn from this story? A bowl of stew for the birthright blessing sounds foolish knowing the value such a blessing holds. It brings to my mind the parable of the foolish virgins. Compare *Matthew 25:1-13 with Gen 25: 29-34*

[Gen 25:29-34 ESV] 29 Once when Jacob was cooking stew, ... ***30 And Esau said to Jacob, "Let me eat some of that red stew,*** *for I am exhausted!" ... 31 Jacob said,* ***"Sell me your birthright now."*** *32 Esau said,* ***"I am about to die; of what use is a birthright to me?"*** *33 Jacob said, "Swear to me now." So he swore to him and sold his birthright to Jacob. 34 Then Jacob gave Esau bread and lentil stew, and he ate and drank and rose and went his way. Thus Esau despised his birthright.*

Imagine giving away something of great value like your 401K plan or a sizable inheritance worth hundreds of thousands to millions of dollars for a single meal. *Note what Esau says to Jacob at Gen 25:32; "I'm about to die, of what use is a birthright to me?"* Apparently, he didn't think he could **LIVE** without the one bowl of stew, feeling he would **DIE** at that instance without it.

He lived in the moment not considering he would later regret his actions, a decision that would have irreversible consequences. *Gen 25:32* That is the way of the world today. Esau's decision was selfish in not considering what he was taking from his offspring. Sometimes, we may feel like Esau, feeling tomorrow may never come. Like Esau, we may **LIVE ONLY** to feed our flesh at all costs, while ruining our lives and others. As mature Christians, we have rejected this Esau spirit that we are all susceptible to. If not, we must change if we are truly dedicated people of God. The **Me** generation feels no price is too high to pay for instantaneous pleasures at the cost of forfeiting everything they have of value. Whatever feels good in the moment is all that matters. Under the first born law Esau would have inherited the blessings of Abraham which would include both material and spiritual prosperity. Esau's god was his belly which represents the lusts of the flesh. People of this mentality may have much regard for material prosperity while disregarding altogether spiritual prosperity. Our spiritual inheritance holds more value than any amount of material gain. God so loved the world that He gave his only begotten Son that whosoever might believe in him would have eternal life. That's spiritual prosperity, this is the blessing of Abraham. Appreciation of our spiritual inheritance leads us to not only love God but love his commandments including everything he stands for. But, the Esau generation considers God's righteous laws and principles irrelevant and burdensome.

If they only knew, it's quite the opposite. However, they're blinded by the god of this world. They worship money instead of the true God to satisfy their greed and lust for material things like fancy cars and homes, food, sex, and entertainment. They would rather spend their time, day in and day out in front of a TV or computer screen to watch immoral programming and pornography while overeating and getting drunk on alcohol. The selfie revolution has taken a hold of mankind making it the most **LOVELESS, CLUELESS** world society ever. Angela Bassett once asked the question, "What's love got to do with it?" I would say everything! Wouldn't you say **LOVING** God is everything because we owe our very existence to HIM. Astonishingly, there's something more at play here. Yes, God wants to teach us another valuable object lesson that will help us appreciate how profound His **LOVE** is for us indeed.

Below is a small portion of a blog posting titled, [6]**"The Blessing of the Firstborn"** by Rick McFarland from Charis Bible College's website.

"There is a pattern with the patriarchs of the Bible. The patriarchs are the men to whom God gave His covenant of grace before the Law. These men included Abraham, Isaac, Jacob, Joseph, and Ephraim. God chose to make a covenant of grace and blessing with Abraham and his seed. It is interesting to follow how this blessing was passed down from Abraham to his descendants.

The family blessing in the ancient world usually went to the firstborn. They had the birthright and the family blessing due them. However, when we follow the blessing of Abraham being passed down, we see a consistent pattern where the firstborn was rejected so that the younger child would receive the blessing of the firstborn. In each case, this firstborn blessing was given to those to whom it was not owed and to those who were undeserving to receive it:

Ishmael was rejected, and Isaac received the blessing.

Esau was rejected, and Jacob received the blessing.

Reuben was rejected, and Joseph received the blessing.

Manasseh was rejected, and Ephraim received the blessing.

Why was this pattern repeated generation after generation? *It was to show us that God's blessing comes by grace and not by merit.* God the Father had a firstborn Son—Jesus. He went to the cross for our sin and was rejected on the cross. *He cried out "My God! My God! Why have you forsaken me?"*

The answer was so that the blessing would come upon the younger—you and me—who did not earn it or deserve it!"

Praise God! [6]The Blessing of the Firstborn | Charis Bible College

HalleluYAH! That sums up everything precisely, doesn't it? Everything leads us to Christ who was rejected for our sake. His sacrifice has given us many blessings in this life and more in the life to come. Yes, now we are blessed to be set free from the bondages of sin which held **Esau** captive. Like Jacob, we are loved by God and not rejected as Esau. The veil has been torn giving us direct access to God the Father through Jesus. How grateful am I for Jesus who opened the way for these blessings of grace, His unmerited favor? Are you as well, beloved? We should never stop asking ourselves this question because we could get caught up in the endtime's **HYPER GRACE** movement. *Romans 6:22, 9:13 Luke 23:45*

The End time's Hyper Grace Movement

What exactly is hyper-grace you may be asking. Simply put it's taking the gift of grace for granted. Like Esau, we're all deserving of God's displeasure. Knowing this moves me to appreciate how much the beloved son of God paid for us to gain God's favor. And now we're called His beloved. This profound love of God moves my heart to love Him as much as I possibly can. Hyper-grace teaches that you can do no wrong in God's eyes, therefore there's no need to repent, no need to turn away from the sins of flesh. It promotes the notion that because our sins are forgiven, past, present and future, there's no sin that can separate us from God. But is this really true? The bible teaches that we SHOULD repent of our sins.

Jesus Christ spoke to the churches in Revelation about the

need to repent. He specifically told the Laodicean church if they didn't repent he would take away their white clothing making them naked, covered in shame. *Rev 3:18-19* This shows a side of His sternness yet notice how profound the Lord's love is for us. He never gives up on us when we go astray. He would much rather administer loving correction, giving us fair warning through straight forward counsel and rebuke. This is a time of fair warning for all of mankind, the church and the world.

Hyper-graced minded people may find themselves facing His rod of discipline which could become necessary, none of which would be easy to take. Discipline never feels good though it comes from the Lord's loving hand. It's clear to me that we are not to take sin lightly just because we know that we overcome by His precious blood. We must also remember to work out our salvation with fear and trembling. One such way is by carefully dividing the Word correctly as we study it within its proper context. Compare *2 Tim 2:15 and Rev 3:18-19 with Phil 2:12-15*

[Phil 2:12-15 KJV] 12 Wherefore, my beloved, as ye have always obeyed, not as in my presence only, but now much more in my absence, **work out your own salvation with fear and trembling.** 13 For it is God which worketh in you both to will and to do of [his] good pleasure. .....: 15 That ye may be **blameless and harmless, the sons of God, without rebuke <u>in the midst of a crooked and perverse nation, among whom ye shine as lights in the world;</u>**

What Does Real Love Require Of Us?

We don't want to face the rebuke of God like Esau. Although he sought God's face with heavy tears of sorrow, it was too late because he didn't appreciate the value of the treasure he had with his birthright. When we look at the text, it says Esau **despised** his birthright. **Despise** *means to hate, feeling repulsive or contempt for something seen as worthless.* True Christians feel quite the opposite of Esau. Through Jesus, we have each been gifted with a priceless inheritance of birthright blessings. Do you remember living in sin, a life of selfish pursuits? I do. We've all been forgiven for many things, some of us more than others. *Phil 2:12 tells us* working out our salvation with fear and trembling comes out of our obedience.Not because someone is watching; we LOVE God for His goodness and mercies which leads us to godly fear and respect. The next verse 13, helps us appreciate how God looks upon those who live a life fully dedicated to Him. He looks upon us with favor as He himself helps us to do good in what's pleasing to Him where we fall short. Glory to God!!! After all God has done for us, how can we not love Him. Consider what God loves and hates. To love Him means loving what He loves, things of righteousness and holiness which motivates us to love and obey His commandments. *Dan 9:4-5* He loves the cheerful giver, those who love their neighbor. He loves you and I so, comforting us like both a loving mother and father, a husband, a wife, a friend, brother or sister, etc. *2Cor 9:7 1Kings 10:9 Matthew 12:50 Isaiah*

66:11-13 Yet, we are challenged to live amidst a perverse and crooked generation, the **Esau generation**. Let your light shine brothers and sisters. Shine in the midst of this **DARK** world by hating evil as much as the Lord does. What He hates speaks of what our love for Him requires of us. He hates a divorce without proper cause, adultery and fornication, every form of sexual immorality, sexual abuse, verbal and physical abuse, lying tongues, greed, and murder. As a matter of emphasis I'd like to reiterate that He has a special affinity for those who love keeping his commandments. *John 14:21 Prov 6:16-19 Malachi 2:16 James 4:8 Rom 13:13*

[Proverbs 6:16-19 NIV] 16 There are six things the LORD hates, seven that are detestable to him: 17 haughty eyes, a lying tongue, hands that shed innocent blood, 18 a heart that devises wicked schemes, feet that are quick to rush into evil, 19 a false witness who pours out lies and a person who stirs up conflict in the community.

Yes, loving and hating what God does will draw us closer to Him. The sheep remain drawn to the Great Shepherd by His gentle touch and loving spirit. They appreciate His loving compassionate voice when He speaks to them through His indwelling spirit. Am I imitating His love and compassion for mankind in general and towards my brothers and sisters in the faith? His true disciples will be known by the love they have among themselves. Is the sanctity of life important to me, whether it's for the living or the unborn inside a woman's womb? Do I have empathy, a special kind of compassion for the poor and needy, the orphans and widows, all those that are disenfranchised in this world? *See John 13:35* As an African American woman, I'm saddened by the pattern of young men in our neighborhoods killing one another at alarming rates across our country. *1 John 2:3-10* There's no surprise in that there's no sanctity for life in the world. Violence and murder are on the rise among all races and walks of life. Wasn't violence a major problem in Noah's day before the flood? There's no respect for life. Judgment has now come upon the church to judge whether it's conducting itself accordingly to God's righteous principles. *1Thess 4:10*

The church must set the example of what genuine love for ALL people should look like. **We hate the sin but we must LOVE the sinner, Amen.** *1 Peter 4:17 Isaiah 58:6-8* The bible says God will judge those on the outside in His own timing. *1Cor 5:12-13 Rev 20:12* **In the end God's kingdom will correct everything that's out of order.** As Christians, love should motivate us to warn the wicked of the coming fiery judgment God will bring, hoping they will repent and turn away from their immoral lifestyles. We must not be afraid to speak the plain truth, we can do it with love and kindness, with a measure of salt. We can share the gospel by lifting up Christ in a way that easily starts a conversation.

We were once in bondage to sin ourselves before submitting our lives to the Lord. Amen *Col 4: 5-6 Ezek 33: 8-9 James 4:8 John 14:15, 21*

Come Out Of The World My People

As the battle rages on, we must persevere, enduring to the end. The victorious, those who overcome will have special privileges granted to them. The church of Philadelphia is promised protection at the time of God's wrath. *Rev 3:10* tells us Jesus Himself will protect us now as we live our lives abiding in Him and get us through to the end. When and how that will be played out entirely remains to be seen. I remain hopeful to endure till the end because we have the blessed hope of the Lord's return which some call the rapture. *Titus 2:13* Moreover, what's worthy of consideration is that our Saviour knows it's not easy for us to stand for holiness in this evil **Esau** generation, the **ME** generation.

Yes, we must leave behind the world, spiritual Egypt and Sodom in order to persevere to the end. Sometimes that may require leaving some people behind. If family, friends, or anyone we may come in contact with wants to engage in worldly things we don't have to participate. It may be something you once enjoyed doing perhaps. Now they may not like the new you but that's not your problem. Also, we can't lose sight of what is most important in this time of the end which is the work of saving lost souls.

How can we save them if we can't save ourselves? Are we setting the right example? The Lord will bless those who put the kingdom first by availing themselves to work in the harvest. God will not take us for granted so we shouldn't take His grace for granted.

Coming out of the world means resisting things that feed our flesh which is why we have to crucify our flesh daily, to come out of Babylon the Great. We must honor the Lord in everything we do, not ourselves. *Amos 5:14-15* If you're not sure of what coming out of the world looks like, you will appreciate how the NLT breaks it down for us here below.

1 John 2:15-17 says, *15 Do not love this world nor the things it offers you, for when you love the world, you do not have the love of the Father in you. 16 For the world offers only a craving for physical pleasure, a craving for everything we see, and pride in our achievements and possessions. These are not from the Father, but are from this world. 17 And this world is fading away, along with everything that people crave. But anyone who does what pleases God will live forever.*

Amen, that says it all. The world is all about promoting self. Keeping up with the latest everything, especially what others have. Competition for the sole purpose of self exaltation is idolized in the world. It has creeped inside the church. Have we examined ourselves having made the decision to come out of Babylon yet? Time's ticking away. God loves us so much. We are all his children.

The people of the world don't see us as children of God because they don't know him. *1 John 3:1* But we know Him being assured many blessings are in store for us. The overcomers of the church of Philadelphia will have the special honor of being pillars inside of the sanctuary of God. *Matt 24:14 1 Peter 2:2-4* That sounds like a super special honor and unique privilege given to them for their faithful service in this life. *Rev 3:12* Paraphrasing Jesus, *Rev 3:8b* says, *'I know you're tired but that's ok with me because you've obeyed me by persevering and you didn't deny my name'.* Glory to God! God knows I'm tired of this evil world. How about you? *1 John 4:17* Our strength must come from the JOY we have in Him, not the things of this world. Things of the world are passing away. Jesus understands the struggles of living in a world surrounded by evil on all sides. His understanding of the battles we are faced with everyday in this hostile world is encouraging. That's wonderful isn't it? No wonder He's called **"Wonderful Counselor"**. *Isaiah 9:6* God's Spirit living inside the heart of each born again believer confirms that we are the true sons of God. *Rom 8:14*

Our holy lifestyle is simply a testimony of our love for the Lord as we anticipate His coming. It will be soon!

Looking Beneath the Surface

Knowing the Lord intimately deepens our appreciation on many levels. Loving God requires our time and effort. We know that David was close to God, writing many psalms about his profound love and intimate relationship with the Lord.

[2 Samuel 6:15-16, 21 NLT] 15 So David and all the people of Israel brought up the Ark of the LORD with shouts of joy and the blowing of rams' horns. 16 But as the Ark of the LORD entered the City of David, **Michal,** *the daughter of Saul, looked down from her window. When* **she saw King David leaping and dancing before the LORD, she was filled with contempt for him**. *... 21 David retorted to Michal, "***I was dancing before the LORD,*** who chose me above your father and all his family! He appointed me as the leader of Israel, the people of the LORD, so I celebrate before the LORD.*

We can learn several lessons about King David and his wife Michal from *2Sam 6:15-17,21* cited above. First of all, we can see He was thankful and grateful for having been called and chosen to rule and reign as the King of Israel. Gratitude moved David to dance, sing and praise the Lord often. One particular day David came home celebrating the arrival of the ark of the covenant with the people, but his wife had contempt in her heart for Him. David's wife Michal, daughter of King Saul, was extremely jealous of David's LOVE for the Lord. Likely knowing the God of Israel dethroned her father in favor of David incited her to jealousy. She despised seeing David praise God feeling irritated.

As Michal looked out the window seeing King David jumping around, she accused Him of showing off for the ladies that were there celebrating with Him. Paraphrasing, I appreciate His response to her saying, **I was dancing before the Lord for the Lord. Because of HIM, I AM BLESSED.**

Loving God Like David

David's unabandoned worship of God drew sharp criticism from Michal. She said he was doing it for attention. In church, some may judge you thinking your unabandoned worship is for attention or show. Perhaps Michal, David's wife would have joined in with Him had she had her own personal relationship with God, if only she would have asked David to share with her more about His God. Then maybe, just maybe she would have understood how great God is and worthy to be praised. She would have been blessed herself to know the ark of the covenant represented the very presence of God among them which is what David was celebrating. Have you ever been around someone who becomes visibly agitated when you start to take the conversation to a spiritual place? You want to talk about the love of God, His goodness, the goodness of heaven, our future home, about the JOYS that are set ahead for us. It doesn't really bother me to see or hear others praising the Lord in any way they want to express themselves, I love it because I understand why they are praising Him.

It's all about Him. I'm not ashamed to praise HIM in front of others. But I wasn't always bold or brave enough to fully express my love for God in front of others at church. And frankly, sometimes you don't feel well for whatever reason. We never know what it takes for someone to make it to church but God knows. Insecurities can hold one back from outwardly expressing their love for God in church service. But it can also be a lack of heartfelt connection to the Lord. It takes time and effort to experience growth in developing our relationship with God. The best way to get to know someone is by spending time with them and communication is key. The Holy Spirit plays a big role in moving us to actively worship God if we are in tune, communicating with Him. There's so many other things that could factor in as to why we don't always raise our hands, or dance, sing and shout with others at church service. I've learned that we are each at different spiritual levels. Time allowed me to grow and strengthen my relationship with the Lord as I increased in knowledge and understanding of Him.

The more I got to know Him, the more intense my love grew which naturally solidified my dedication to Him. I sat for too many years in a church where it was not okay to say 'halleluyah" or "praise the Lord". You were expected to keep silent during the sermon and only listen. After over 20 years God brought me out of this denomination where I was slowly dying a spiritual death. He revived my spirit with the Holy Spirit which set me free to express my love openly for God.

Now if I'm in a church where unabandoned worship is not their thing, I can feel out of place. I LOVE LOVE LOVE openly expressing my love for the King of Kings like King David. Glory to God! Yes indeed, if we remain on the right path and seek God with all our heart, spending time in the secret place, we will come to the place that David was at in his worship of God. And guess what? That place of unabandoned worship doesn't always have to be at a church gathering, it just may be in your car, at the store, on a street corner or in the privacy of your home. I've come to the conclusion that David had two major keys: **Dedication** and **Meditation.** David was fully dedicated to the Lord and always meditated upon the goodness of God.

He knew the Lord well and we can appreciate the glorious picture he paints for us of the Lord. Just like David, I can't help but praise Him knowing the ark of God's presence is within me. David's beautiful poetic expressions of his profound love for the Lord are timeless treasures. I was not planning to write about this so perhaps someone reading this needed to hear this. Bottom line is we shouldn't make judgements about people when it comes to the way they express their worship or lack of expression for God in church or any public setting. It's one thing to encourage others to worship and another when we try to force it and talk down to them when they don't respond. I would think one can be strong in the Lord and not display their emotions openly for whatever reasons.

Whatever the reasons, they're between them and God alone. What gives me the right to measure my act of worship against yours. I can't read what's inside of your heart. Remember Hannah who sat quietly in the sanctuary with the priest. She wanted to have a child after being barren for many years. The bible tells us that one day Hannah was in the house of the Lord praying silently and the high priest mistakenly thought she was drunk when he saw her lips moving but there was no sound coming from her mouth. Our dialogue with God does not always have to be out loud. Hanna was in anguish over being childless. I'm not sure exactly how long her prayer went unanswered but hope deferred does make the heart sick. However, the Lord answered her specific silent prayer request giving her a son a year later. That son was the prophet Samuel. *1 Samuel 1:2-20* It's possible the quiet one seated in your church, not shouting and praising God out loud is praising and worshiping Him inside of their heart. Like Hannah, maybe they're in anguish over some pressing matter they've been praying about. My prayer is that if you are not prone to publicly express what's in your heart for God, know that the Lord does hear your silent prayers of petition, and your silent praise and worship. He reads what's stored inside of your heart. Besides, being **SHY** or **ANXIOUS,** preoccupation with **WORRY, or feeling ill or sad,** that's not the same as **someone feeling ASHAMED of the Lord and the good news of the Gospel. Amen**

Our Light Must Shine In The Darkness

*We live at a time of dense spiritual darkness when our lamps need to be full of oil to light our pathway leading to our heavenly Father and our Lord Jesus Christ. Am I a wise or foolish virgin? Am I short on oil and if so, why? How and where do I get my oil? How do I keep an overflow supply? What happens if I wait until the last minute and there's no oil left in the lamp? Do I ask a wise virgin for some of their oil? These are all good questions that I will try to answer. I asked the Lord why did the wise virgins tell the foolish virgins to go and buy oil, wasn't it free? After thinking about it, this is my own take on what happened. The wise virgins knew what was up with the foolish virgins.

In my opinion, the wise virgins answer was really a rhetorical answer. It's like this, you ask me a stupid question, I give you a stupid answer. As **PRECIOUS** as the **OIL** is, why would I give it away to you when you had **ACCESS** to the **FREE FLOW of OIL** as I did. In other words the wise virgins knew the foolish **had enough time and the knowledge** to know how to get extra oil for themselves. So their lack of oil was due to their own selfishness, laziness, and foolish behavior. The Lord did begin to speak to me and answer my question. He helped me to understand that though the OIL is **FREE** flowing, the oil does cost us something. The currency to buy the oil is not the usual currency of money.

The currency to purchase the oil is called **TIME, the most valuable currency of today. TIME is a free gift** from the Lord to everyone. Each day we wake up with the breath of life from God, we are given more time free of charge. That makes the oil we can purchase with time free. However, what must be weighed in the analysis of this parable are several variables which determine whether we are one of the foolish or wise virgins. The clincher here is found in how the currency of time is spent. It can be used to purchase many other things besides the much needed **OIL** in our illustration. Rationally we can conclude that the foolish virgins expended their time pursuing their own thing rather than the things of God.

The foolish virgins were unwise for not seeking the Lord getting to know him intimately or personally. Both the foolish and the wise virgins had the Word of God at their disposal. Only the wise however used their time wisely, time being the **ONLY** currency needed to purchase the extra oil. The time came when both the wise and foolish virgins' time ran out when the bridegroom arrived. The foolish sadly had nothing left to purchase the extra oil needed to light their lamps and see their way in a dark world. Their lights were going out. Before they were healthy vines attached to the olive tree but their branches became detached and were dying. The most obvious and simple answer of this parable is that the oil represents the Holy Spirit. Yet it goes much deeper than that.

The oil which is the Holy Spirit is found in the Word, the written Word of God, the Holy Bible and in the living Word, Jesus Christ. They both go hand in hand. We live in a complex world which puts a lot of demands on our time. The wise virgins utilized their currency of TIME to buy out time from their busy schedule to study and meditate on the Word of God, thereby receiving an impartation of God's Holy Spirit which is Christ in us, the living Word. As we study and meditate on the Word, we come to know Jesus as a person and we are able to develop a close personal relationship with him and the Father and the Holy Spirit. Time is of the essence when it comes to buying out the **opportune time** for ourselves. Why? Because the days are wicked. The Lord will soon return and he will come as a thief to those who are not paying attention and not ready. They're unprepared with no oil in their lamps. The darkness of this world will overtake them because they have either gone back to sleep, or are drunk on the maddening wine of this world which can lead to sickness and depression. Being low or completely out of oil will hinder your ability to keep going in a dark world such as this. What could be signs we are running low or out of oil? Possibly, if you can't see any hope in your future at all, feeling everything is hopeless, you're either low on oil or even more so completely out of oil. We pointed out that the oil is the Holy Spirit. The Holy Spirit is a person. The bible calls him the **"Comforter"**. He's my best friend who leads me in the way.

We follow his lead in this dark world which will ultimately lead us to the day of Christ's return or the end of our life. When we are filled with Him, the fruits will manifest in our lives and the spirit is what keeps us going.

He is a comforter when times get really hard while we're going through severe trials, testings and persecutions. One fruit of the spirit is **"JOY"**. If we lack joy of the spirit we know we are running low and possibly completely out of oil. Jesus knew we would get tired, feel hard pressed to the point of wanting to give up altogether. This is why he said he would leave us with the comforter. Feeling joyful in trying circumstances is unrealistic for us which God understands, therefore he promised he would never put on us more than we can bear. He will sustain us and even give us a JOY that's unspeakable in the midst of severe trials. I have felt so much JOY when under pressure that I knew without a doubt it was the Lord's presence. Peace is another fruit of his spirit. He gives peace that surpasses all understanding. No one really understands how we can feel this immense JOY and PEACE under such trying circumstances that we may be undergoing in this dark world. But only with oil in our lamp will we have the comforter and helper to get us through with the much needed extra oil because the days are wicked.

[Romans 5:1-5 NIV] *"Therefore, since we have been justified through faith, we have PEACE with God through our Lord Jesus Christ, through whom we have gained access by faith into this grace in which we now stand. And we REJOICE in the hope of the glory of God. Not only so, but we also REJOICE in our sufferings, because we know that suffering produces perseverance, perseverance, character, and character hope. And hope does not disappoint us, because God has poured out his love into our hearts by the Holy Spirit, whom he has given us."*

If you feel you have been overflowing with oil at one time and find that you have somehow lost your JOY and PEACE it's possible that you have given all your oil away or just used it all up yourself. It's time to replenish your supply now. We need to open our bibles and read and meditate upon God's promises and draw strength as He imparts His spirit upon us. Also spending time in prayer and communing with the Lord is another way to get more oil. It's imperative we keep an overflow to keep our lamps full and lit in this dark world. We know what happened to those who were out of oil when the Lord came unexpectedly as a thief. Jesus refused to open the door to them and said I don't know you. That's a harsh statement but the truth can be harsh. It's better to be informed now so that we can make wise decisions now that will shape our destiny to be included among the wise virgins.

[Ephesians 5:15-17 NIV] *15 Be very careful, then, how you live--not as unwise but as wise, 16 making the most of every opportunity, because the days are evil. 17 Therefore do not be foolish, but understand what the Lord's will is.*

This is not the time to go back to sleep as is the case likely with some of the foolish virgins. All the virgins heard the call that the bridegroom was coming. They all started out on the same road going out to meet the bridegroom upon his arrival. Are you perhaps wondering what would indicate whether you are spiritually asleep or awake, consider this. Today, those that are awake can see that many things going on in the world are clear signs and signals of the Lord's soon return. So you may now say, oh good I'm AWAKE then. I know what the scriptures say and I can see all the signs. Yes, but is this enough? *1Thess 5:6, Rev 16:15*

[1Thess 5:6 NIV] 6 *"So then, let us not be like others, who are asleep, but let us be awake and sober."*

[Rev 16:15 NIV] 15 *"Look, I come like a thief! Blessed is the one who stays awake and remains clothed so as not to go naked and be shamefully exposed."*

Time for Self-Examination

OK, upon self examination we will recognize whether we are awake or not and must analyze how we are spending our time when awake. There is more to realizing we are awake besides knowing what's happening in the world. The way one spends their AWAKE TIME is the determining factor of whether one is a wise or foolish virgin. The scripture says not only should we stay awake but remain clothed and not go about naked being shamefully exposed.

If one's time is being spent pursuing the things of the world and being entertained by worldly demoralizing entertainment, our currency of time is being wasted. Bad association spoils useful habits. Worldly influence can remove our clothes, our spiritual covering of God's Holy Spirit. *1Cor 15:33 Rev 16:15*

Without the Holy Spirit's help, we lack bearing fruit evidenced by a worldly way of thinking and living, which leads to shame in the presence of God. No oil can be attained in pursuit of a worldly lifestyle. Only maddening wine is what one will get for their currency of time in these pursuits which leads to being spiritually intoxicated, in other words drunk. This maddening wine leads to spiritual ruin, a state of confusion, becoming too weak and tired to do anything related to your spiritual edification. This is why the Lord warns us.

***[Ephesians 5:18 NIV]** 18 Do not get drunk on wine, which leads to debauchery. Instead, be filled with the Spirit, 19 speaking to one another with psalms, hymns, and songs from the Spirit. Sing and make music from your heart to the Lord, 20 always giving thanks to God the Father for everything, in the name of our Lord Jesus Christ.*

Spiritual debauchery is utter ruin. Let us therefore spend time in pursuits that put us in God's presence like singing songs to him from the heart, simply thanking the Lord for all he has done and seeking his spirit. Be WISE with your TIME, the most valuable currency of all. It's worth more than all the gold and silver in the world. We need to buy extra oil to replenish our supply. It's free! The oil is the Holy Spirit! HalleluYAH

It comes from time spent studying the written Word, and the living Word, Jesus Christ. Also, spend time with other wise virgins. The wise virgins recognized the price was small when compared to what they were receiving with their precious currency of time. Having and overflow, it was a currency well spent. Every second of time spent studying and meditating upon the Word, soaking in His presence was well worth it. Our getting to know the Lord means life, everlasting life. See *John 17:3* Don't be one of the FOOLISH virgins where Jesus will close the door and say, I don't know you! Repent! *Matthew 25:10-13* **Morning Manna with Love Blog, "Do I Have Enough Oil To Make It"** *archives 7/31/15*

Holiness Our Most Beautiful Apparel

Every time we fall down, we must get up with genuine heartfelt repentance. There's no condemnation for those in Christ Jesus. *Rom 8:1* Along the way we learn dancing with the King of Kings is a lifelong journey and process of growing in our relationship with the Lord. Enjoy the dance my friends! I'm still dancing with Him today even though I have my challenges. Falling into sin will do that among other things. If it's not deliberate unrepentant sin, we can stay on the right path by sincerely repenting. Grace will empower us to overcome sin.

1 John 3:6 NLT says, "Anyone who continues to live in Christ will not sin. But anyone who keeps on sinning, practicing sin doesn't know Christ or understand who He is".

Reading the Word and meditating on it will increase our love and devotion for God.[9]Prophet Lovy of Revelation Church has a study on how we can read the Word of God effectively. I don't agree with everything he says and I'm not a part of his church ministry but I have watched a few of his videos.

Consider this. What's the point of saying, *'I've read the entire bible in one year'* without it changing my life in at least one profound way. He speaks about how useless it is when one can quote scriptures word for word yet it remains only in our mind. To me he's saying, having head knowledge is meaningless and useless. If it hasn't been stored inside of the heart, head knowledge becomes dead knowledge. We are powerless and fruitless in this frame of mind.

[9]Prophet Lovy went on to say, *'the Word is rhema, God speaking'.* As we meditate planting the Word inside of our heart we will see it come alive with the power of God. It will grow and produce fruit in our life.

I know far too well how sin can draw a wedge in between us and the Lord, especially if it's not dealt with. Old habits are hard to break which Jesus understands. Yet, unrepentant habitual unclean practices, especially sexual sin will grieve the Holy Spirit.

Unrepentance will always hinder our growth and ability to progress in our relationship while dancing with the Lord. It can certainly open the door to the enemy. Remember, God promises to never leave us nor forsake us. The problem's when we leave Him through our own doing. If you've fallen into a pattern of habitual sin, Jesus can and will set you free. Simply repent, be genuine. God will forgive the most hideous of sins including hidden sins. *Psalm 19:12-13*

Ask the Holy Spirit for help but as well as spiritually mature Christians for prayer and advice. Proverbs 1:5

Remember Jesus' blood was shed to cover all of our sins, God's grace gives us hope which strengthens us. Jesus, our intercessor, is totally on our side. God sees us in Christ Jesus as righteous and blameless. With grateful hearts we can rejoice in this, knowing His abiding grace will lead us to worship Him in the beauty of holiness. He's pleased that we want to stand in holiness offering our best, the first fruits of our heart to please Him because we love Him. *2Chron 29:5-6, 28, 31; 30:8 Jer 31:33*

Going Into The Secret Place

The beauty of holiness intensifies as we pursue the Spirit of God in the secret place. Our continual progress in development takes us to a higher place in Him as we meditate on his powerful Word which is able to divide between our soul and spirit ...discerning what is stored in our heart.

See *Hebrews 4:12* Go through the opened door to heaven's throne of grace. When was the last time you went before the throne of grace in the secret place? We can go boldly but it's okay to go in with a humble heart knowing it doesn't minimize who we are in Christ Jesus. Speak the Word in your heart to Him.

[1 Chron 16:29 KJV] 29 Give unto the LORD the glory [due] unto his name: bring an offering, and come before him: **worship the LORD in the beauty of holiness.**

Soaking in the secret place is a good way to start our day talking to God, thanking Him for another day of life, reading a bible passage or something bible based. Feasting on some morning manna along with your coffee and breakfast or whatever your morning routine is, it's a good way to get prepared for the day. I've learned that getting spiritually dressed is the most meaningful thing I can do to start my day out right. We shouldn't go one day without making sure all of our spiritual armor is in place which is provided by the Lord for our protection. *Ephes 6:11-18.* The best way of doing that is never taking your armor off. After COVID 19, I formed a new habit to cover myself with prayer speaking *Psalm 91* declarations and other scriptural proclamations over myself. It doesn't have to be the whole scripture, it can be one verse or two of Psalm 91. God appreciates the simple little things like that when done out of a clean heart. Sometimes it's good to listen to praise and worship music as well. *Rev 3:8*

*[Ephesians 6:18 NLT] 18 **Pray in the Spirit** at all times and on every occasion. Stay alert and be persistent in your prayers for all believers everywhere.*

Praying in the spirit to me is simply communicating with God's Spirit from our spirit through the Holy Spirit, heart to heart. And going in deep may produce groanings as we speak in tongues that only the Spirit understands. *Romans 8:26 We can always ask the Lord what he's saying if we don't understand.* Taking out time for prayer puts me in the right frame of mind to do what God has called me to do. It helps that He's given us the breastplate of righteousness which is a beautiful covering provided by the blood of the Lamb. Without holiness no one will see God. Do you appreciate the value of our spiritual armor, our **beautiful apparel of holiness**? When we discern some piece of armor is missing, we must examine ourselves to find out what it is.

*[Hebrews 12:14 NIV] 14 Make every effort to live in peace with everyone and to be holy; **without holiness no one will see the Lord.***

It's not about earning our salvation. The blood of the Lamb guarantees salvation which means eternal life is free. I've found for myself that inside the secret place we are strengthened and given gifts of the Holy Spirit. All we have to do is ask. It's a place of intimate heartfelt communication with God. Tell God how much you want more of Him. Go after Him with the zeal and fire of your heart.

Next submit fully to the process of His transforming power. As I've said before, transformation isn't always easy, but we have a helper, the Holy Spirit and spiritually qualified men and women of God to assist us in the renewal and transformational process. God wants us to come for help without any fears when we need to. That means relying on his strength and power. In Christ alone is the victory to prevail and persevere in our spiritual battles. *Psalm 54:4 Heb 13:6 Isa 55:3 John 7:37*

[Rev 3:10 NLT] 10 "Because you have obeyed my command to persevere, I will protect you from the great time of testing that will come upon the whole world ....

Our Covenant Relationship

Do you see God's amazing love for those fully dedicated and devoted to Him, determined to persevere at all costs when under trials? I always sense that He's excited, knowing that His **FAITHFUL future BRIDE,** a remnant church will be ready when He returns for her. No, she's not perfect in works, but the Holy Spirit is. In the Jewish culture, a man and woman engaged to be married are in a covenantal marital relationship that can only be broken except by a divorce.

So it is with the church bride. She's engaged, promised in marriage, in a covenant relationship with Christ. *2Cor 11:2* Although the wedding of the bride and bridegroom is still yet to come, she's already married to Him spiritually in her heart.

Therefore it's appropriate to speak of Christ and the faithful church as bride and bridegroom. Compare *Rev 19:7-9* The Lord leads and guides her along the straight and narrow path of life. He's our helper working to keep our abiding heart **PURE**, **PERFECTLY** aligned and **COMPLETE** in **HIM if we allow Him to**. The bride doesn't practice sin because she abides in Jesus, the true vine. *John 15:9-11, Ephes 3:16-20*

For this reason He imputes His righteousness to her, giving her **FINE WHITE LINEN** to wear. Because she's led by the Holy Spirit, her righteous works come natural as she abides in the love stemming from the law of love written inside of her heart. Love covers a multitude of sins. If you listen closely you can hear the **HOLY SPIRIT** whisper how much **HE LOVES YOU**. Have you come to know God intimately? We are the most blessed people in the whole **UNIVERSE**, because to know Him is to **LOVE** Him. To know Him means I KNOW how much He LOVES ME. *Psalm 91, 139* I can **REST in HIM because He's my SABBATH rest, my FORTRESS and REFUGE in whom I trust, my BEST FRIEND, my HUSBAND** ....my everything. *Psalm 18:2; 20:6, Isaiah 55:5, John 15:13, 15   Song 1:5, 1Cor 2:7-16*

Delightful Manna in Spiritual Intimacy

Recall the Holy Spirit descended upon Jesus in the form of a dove when he was baptized by John the baptizer? *John 1:32* The beautiful faithful bride of Christ has been endowed with the Holy Spirit which explains the bridegroom seeing his bride with the **eyes of doves.** *Song 1:15* How positive we feel about ourselves is a reflection of what we see when we look into our eyes, a mirror for the soul. Do we see the love of Christ looking back at us or do we see fruits of darkness like shame, guilt, anger, bitterness, selfishness, laziness, sexual immorality, greed, etc.? I remember times I didn't see His love inside my eyes. Instead I saw emptiness and darkness. I know I have problems with anger, pride, selfishness and unclean thoughts but God. God knows whether our heart is pure or not and if we're honest with ourselves we'll see our real self. Like the psalmist prayed, we must pray for God to examine our heart and reveal what is not right in His sight. That's why I'm so grateful for the secret place because it's there I can come clean before God appreciating how Christ has transferred me into HIS marvelous light. *2Cor 10:13* Everyday my goal is to draw near to God by His grace provided by the **blood of the Lamb.** *Psalm 73:28* There are times the darkness may creep back in but we can cast the darkness out bringing the light back in. Jesus is our helper and friend. Amen *Hebrews 9:28 1 Peter 1:2,19-21*

[Ephes 2:12-13 NLT] 1 12 In those days you were living apart from Christ. You were excluded from citizenship among the people of Israel, ... You lived in this world without God and without hope. 13 But now you have been united with Christ Jesus. Once you were far away from God, **but now you have been brought near to him through the blood of Christ.**

Yes, the light helps us to see the contents of our heart. Naturally we want to see godly qualities within ourselves when we look into the mirror of our soul. When we see mostly works of the flesh after examination, we know what to do. As we draw near living by the power of the Holy Spirit, His spirit gives us wisdom to walk circumspectly, as we examine ourselves with the Word of God to discern what is or isn't pleasing to the Lord. Abiding in the light reflects the beauty of holiness which manifests fruits of the Holy Spirit. May the light always shine brightly within us. It will if Christ is truly in us.

Residing in the Secret Place

[Song 1:2-4 ESV] 2 [She] **Let him kiss me with the kisses of his mouth! For your love is better than wine;** *3 your anointing oils are fragrant; your name is oil poured out; ... 4 Draw me after you; ....* **The king has brought me into his chambers.** *[Others] We will exult and rejoice in you; we will extol your love more than wine; rightly do they love you.*

The shulamite maiden loves to be kissed by the King and so does the faithful bride love the kisses of the bridegroom. How does it feel when Jesus gives you a kiss? *Song 1:2*

I'm speaking about spiritual intimacy, when the kisses of Jesus **MOUTH** are pleasant delightful **WORDS** spoken to His faithful bride in His WORD. All of His sheep know His voice answering His call to intimacy as they enter the King's chamber by His invitation. This place of spiritual intimacy is comparable to the place I like to call the tabernacle of my heart. I love hearing the Lord's voice by means of His Spirit speaking to my soul through the scriptures, anointed words spoken to be stored in my mind and heart. Today in Christ we can experience the peace of God which flows like a powerful yet peaceful river leading to the joy felt by His anointed presence. Imagine floating, soaking and swimming in this river of peace which leads to immeasurable **JOY.** Experiencing the power of His peaceful presence assures us that we have a future of eternal rest in Him. For certain, God wants a close relationship with each one of His brides now and forever.

Your time and experience in the secret place may be expressed differently than it has been for me. I can only tell you about my dance with the King of Kings. One day I realized what was most important to Him when I learned that He had a special assignment for me which I grew to cherish and truly love. The most significant part of my assignment is the same work assignment each and every Christian believer is called for, to make disciples, to seek and save the lost and deliver those in bondage. *Matthew 24:14, 28:19-20*

[Song 6:2-3 KJV] 2 My beloved is gone down into his garden,.. the beds of spices, to feed in the gardens, and **to gather lilies.** 3 **I am my lover's, and my lover is mine.** *He browses among the lilies.*

Yes, many are called but few are chosen. Taking care of the lilies in the field is what makes our bridegroom's heart glad. It took some time but the shulamite maiden finally came to realize that the way to the King's heart was working side by side with Him in the field gathering lilies. *Matthew 22:14*

I learned to appreciate this too as I spent time with Him inside the tabernacle, the inner place of communion, the place where the Holy Spirit dwells inside of our heart. It's there inside the heart He teaches and comforts us, but sometimes He corrects us with measured words that may hurt but it's done in love to lighten the sting of discipline. Therefore, going inside the tabernacle I always expect to learn something about myself and most importantly, something about God. The more time I spent studying the gospels, the more my heart was moved to go share the gospel of Christ with my neighbors. As I came to know Jesus I could hear His still small voice which is how I learned all about my calling and purpose in life. There in the secret place He planted inside of me a profound love for all people. I love that the bridegroom sacrificed His life for all of mankind, not just for a few. We're His **BELOVED** and He's our **BELOVED**. That kind of love draws me in each day as it continually grows inside of me.

We will love spending time with the Lord, soaking in His presence as we engage in deep bible study and/ or meditation or any activity of interest to Him. *Psalm 104:34* Gaining knowledge about end time mysteries and listening to the audio bible are a few of my greatest passions. Evangelist Dorothy Ellis, a dear friend, described to me one day how precious intimate time with the Lord was to her. *"Many times, she said, I'm up til the break of dawn not realizing how much time I've spent in the Word until I see the sun rising". 'Yes, time flies, I said, when you're having fun'.* Her words sounded so familiar. At times I've spent hours reading or listening to the bible, studying without getting tired to gain wisdom and understanding. It's a sacred space, one treasured by all truth seekers, the place we enter when we read and study the bible. The Word is so enjoyable to read or listen to, tasting, Oh so good. You just can't get enough of it because it's food for the soul. *Compare Proverbs 4:7, 16:16*

Arise In Holy Sanctification

Holy is the God we serve, Amen. We must be holy as He is holy. God understands we are born in sin but unrepentant sin of any kind is wrong. Furthermore, unrepentant sexual sin is in a different class all of its own. We know that immoral behavior is detrimental to our spiritual well being, because it demoralizes character, and our spiritual covering. But, what is it about sexual sin that distinguishes it into a class all by itself?

[1Cor 6:19-20 ESV] 19 Or do you not know that **your body is a temple of the Holy Spirit within you**, whom you have from God? You are not your own, 20 for you were bought with a price. So glorify God in your body.

Perhaps, it's because we're all members of the BODY of Christ. Whomever we join ourselves with, we become one with them. The apostle Paul likens sexual sin as becoming one with a prostitute. This is why we are told to **FLEE** from fornication or any type of sexual immorality.

"Every other sin a person commits is outside the body, but the sexually immoral person sins against his own body." 1Cor 6: 18

Yes, sexual sin is sinning **against** our body which is the temple of the Holy Spirit. We must remember we no longer belong to ourselves, but to God in Christ and the members of the body of Christ. Jesus bought us for a hefty price, by His precious blood. Sexual immorality has a way of breaking our spirit in a way that makes us feel ashamed, vulgar, defiled and dirty, that's if we have a conscience. *1Cor 6:14-20* God wants us to be pure in mind and heart, humble and child-like by relying on the strength only He can provide through a Father's loving hand. He'll help us to resist any unclean desires of our flesh. Today inside of the church lurks seducing spirits which are demons of lust. Their objective is to get you and I to fall captive to any sin but in this case we're speaking about sexual sin. To show you how prevalent these kinds of seducing spirits of sexual sin are, you can go on YT and find hundreds if not thousands of videos about seducing spirits inside of the churches.

They come subtly meaning quietly and yet sometimes bold and brazenly. If you all of a sudden start feeling sexual sensations out of the blue, doing nothing to bring it on, more than likely you are dealing with seducing spirits. Not always of course, sometimes it could be hormones. But you will know which it is if you are in tune with yourself coupled with spiritual discernment. One day I was watching a minister's bible prophecy conference on YT, someone I have great respect for because his teachings are profoundly in depth and seem to always be scripturally sound. I listened to one of his guest speakers, a minister and gifted musician who appeared to be well respected in the charismatic Pentecostal churches. He's known for his anointed music and prophetic dreams. Always test the spirit to make sure anyone including me is being led by the Holy Spirit. Everyone has a measure of spiritual discernment because why else would God say test the spirits if we couldn't get reliable results from His indwelling Holy Spirit. On this video the man of God began giving his testimony about an encounter he had with the Holy Spirit. I will try to paraphrase what was said. He spoke about one night during his worship time, when out of nowhere he started feeling sensations, saying it felt like when he's being intimate with his wife. He went as far as moving his body in circular motions, demonstrating for us his experience as though having relations with his wife. He said in so many words that this had been a wonderful experience with the Holy Spirit.

Of course my mouth dropped open as I listened to this. I couldn't believe what I was seeing and hearing. A few years later I went back and found that video because I was thinking surely someone would have said something to him by now, prompting him to remove it. To my surprise it was still uploaded on YT. I found out other Christians were having similar experiences seeking freedom from this bondage from hell. But it's obvious that many are okay with it. Evidently today these seducing spirits are thriving inside of churches, proven by the loads of websites, books, articles, videos and social media posts online addressing this issue. That is a testament to the enormity of this growing problem that's challenging the church. Who knows how many in the churches feel like this brother I just described here, that's it's okay. I'm no judge, just writing as the Lord leads me to expose this dirty little secret. So many others have also been led to openly discuss this issue . For all I know he may now have come to a change of heart. The silence and/or toleration of these spirits of lust inside the churches are prompting a lot of God's people to speak out against it because it is so prevalent. Amen. I've experienced these lust demons myself so I'm speaking from personal experience. You're left feeling so dirty and ashamed and guilty. I later came to understand God knows this was not of my doing, I didn't ask for any of it, it would happen without my invitation.

It almost always happened when I was writing a song, or playing on my keyboard. I finally realized it was for the purpose of distracting me. But God!!! God can help us when we seek His help. They will leave you alone for a while and then come back later to test you. They sometimes come in my dreams and it's nothing I'm doing to bring it on. I live clean and holy as a single woman but the enemy wants to soil my covering as well as every Christian. A great deal of my ministry is focused on spiritual intimacy with the Most High in Christ Jesus because He is our present helper and friend. He may lead some to Christian counseling. It can be the key for those who need someone to walk it out with them in getting set free. I've had a hard battle in these things and I still get tested by these spirits, but I have learned how to fight and resist them with the Lord's help. You must never let your guard down ever. Prayer, bible study, and checking your spiritual armor is a must. *1 Peter 5:7 James 4:9* Keeping the doors of communication opened with someone you trust is also key for some. Never isolate yourself unless it's God's direction for a special purpose. Sometimes He does have us isolated for training and discipline or a special work assignment. For certain, be wise in choosing who you talk to. You don't have to go into great detail with just anyone about such things. Not everyone will understand. There's a lot more I could be saying but wisdom doesn't allow me to give you all the details of my experiences.

I've shared enough to help someone who may be dealing with these types of issues. My book may be the first and only book they will ever read that touches however lightly it does upon this issue.Now they may know for the first time that they are not alone. If you are challenged in this area, I recommend you stay active and engaged with people, especially people who are spiritually mature or progressing in their walk with the Lord. Iron sharpens iron. Find someone to confide in but most of all lay this burden upon the Lord, lean upon him. I did and He has helped me in every way I needed. I can say I'm in a good place today finally understanding how to stand my ground which is to pray, resist, resist, resist and pray, pray, pray. These spirits are all around us waiting to get us to fall in sin. Although sex is a gift from our Creator, sexual perversions are forbidden whether between ourselves alone, between unmarried persons or someone not our spouse if we're married, or persons of the same sex, animals or spirits. *Luke 18:17 Sex was created for the purpose of procreation and also the enjoyment of intimacy between a married couple, a man and woman. Romans 1:24-28*

[Job 28:28 KJV] *28 .. unto man he said, Behold, the fear of the Lord, that [is] wisdom;..depart from evil [is] understanding.*

Sometimes the guilt and shame of feeling something like that when you know where it's coming from can be overwhelming. And to be frank sometimes it's our own feelings that get taken advantage of by the enemy.

They watch us so they know when we're feeling lonely or vulnerable. They know our weaknesses. For this reason what I needed most was to get to the point of repentance, turning my laughter into mourning, my joy into heaviness. There's no condemnation for those that are in Christ Jesus but we have to come to terms in recognizing the gravity of sexual sin or any kind of grievous sin for that matter. *Job 28:28* When we are in Christ, abiding as we should he leads us through the Holy Spirit to repentance. The fear of the Lord is wisdom and to depart from evil is understanding. Amen

There is no shame in being sad or depressed because of sin. After our time of repentance which leads to lamenting, a godly sadness, the blood of Jesus (Yehoshua) sets us free to laugh again and again and again. True repentance means taking concrete steps to protect yourself, to close opened doors that have invited the enemy in. Open doors can be porn, surfing the net, entertaining things of a sexual nature or simply spending too much time online or watching too much TV. Other things like anger, resentment, bitterness, unforgiveness, taking offense, gluttony and greed can all open doors to evil seducing spirits lurking behind your door. Our flesh gets us into trouble. Let's face it, that's the way it is. Sometimes we don't have to go looking for trouble but trouble somehow finds us when we're in the wrong company. Evil company corrupts useful habits.

Awaken to righteousness and do not sin.... *1Cor 15:33-34a* In the end, we have to take full responsibility for our spiritual health and welfare. Sometimes we want to blame someone else for our spiritual condition. For example, sometimes we may be quick to think when we encounter a different spirit attacking us, influencing bad behavior, we want to say it was due to a spirit transferred from so and so. That's possible but sometimes it's not what we thought. In fact, we encounter spirits everywhere, everyday, so the bottom line is that spirits see openings somewhere in us where we are most vulnerable. *James 1:12-14* says, we are all tried by what's **inside** of **us**, **our own lusts of our flesh**. Most often, our issues have nothing to do with anyone else, it wasn't God's fault or anyone else's, it's something we personally need to deal with and correct. Our fight is not against flesh and blood, so stop blaming someone else. *Compare James 1:12-17, 4:1-17, and 5:16 Ephesians 6:12* I had to learn to take full responsibility for my spiritual well being. Sometimes you have to make choices and changes in certain environments. Sometimes your friends won't understand. It's ok, just do what you have to do. Submitting to the cleansing process is part of the bride's preparation of sanctification for the bridegroom. The Holy Spirit will lead us in knowing what we need to do if we are submitted and committed to Him. *Rev 19:7* Queen Esther was a prophetic type of the bride in the Old Testament. She was an orphan, without parents yet God elevated her to the status of Queen.

She was made ready to marry the King by provisions of beauty treatments to prepare her to meet with the King. Her life illustrates how it is God who supplies the provisions for our purification and sanctification process. We are like orphans in this world and Christ adopts us. He wants each one of us in the body of Christ, both men and women to fulfill our unique calling for a time such as this. Those who are faithful to God having the faith of Abraham are called "**BEAUTIFUL**". The faithful bride of Israel is **beautiful** indeed in the Father's eyes because she stands in the **BEAUTY** of His **holiness. HOLY** is His name. *Luke 1:49* Let's take a look at one special Hebrew word for **"beautiful"**. It comes from [9]Strongs Hebrew, **H3303**, *yahpeh'* pronounced **"yah-feh"**, the "e", sounds like long "a", as in say. It sounds like **yah-fay,** sometimes spelled **ya-fe.** I believe this is why the **Most High Yah** had me add the "e" to my name **F**ay**e**, so that hurt little girl could see Abba Father Yah loves her, calling her to testify of His good name inside the four letters of her name. And now I can tell you that He loves you too. This Hebrew word **ya-fe** is translated in the Old Testament **41** times as, **beautiful, fair, and pleasant. FE** means "**FAITH**" in Spanish. In other words, all who put their **FAITH** in **YAH**, the Most High Yah, are **BEAUTIFUL, FAIR, and PLEASANT.**

Amazing how we're perceived by God being connected to Him through His beautiful name. Hallelu**YAH**!!! Praise **YAH**! *Psalm 9:2,10 1 Chronicles 17:24*

King David's Beautiful Countenance

[1Sam 16:12 KJV] *12 And he sent, and brought him in. Now he [was] ruddy, [and] withal of a **beautiful[H3303]** countenance, and goodly to look to. And the LORD said, **Arise, anoint him: for this [is] he.***

David is the ruddy man being described here as **beautiful** using the same word **H3303 yahpeh/"yah-feh"**. The prophet Samuel anointed him as Israel's future king by Yahweh's instruction. The bride of Christ, professes **FAITH** in Israel's present day king, (Yahshua)Jesus , **ANOINTED** by Yahweh. The bride's beautiful countenance is a reflection of Christ the King of Israel's beautiful countenance. Soon the members of the bride class God's elect, Israel will reign with the King of Kings as kings and priests to the glory of Yahweh, the Most High Yah. *Psalm 83:18 Rev 1:6 5:10* Praise God! Savor these nuggets of treasure woven inside of the robe of righteousness gifted to the **beautiful** bride of Christ Messiah today. Overcomers walk in holiness purified by the blood of Christ and sanctified by the Holy Spirit. May we continue to bask in the presence of His radiance. *Rev 12:1 1Peter 2:9* This is the day that the Lord has made, rejoice and be made glad in it because all of Israel will be saved in the end. *Romans 11:26*

Christ' Blood 'is the Substance of our Purification

Holy Spirit 'is the Substance of our Sanctification

Live * Love * Lament * Laugh

Live your life with purpose to the fullest for the Most High Yah. Never give up, and never forget this is a faith walk and dance with the King of Kings.

Love the Most High Yah above all things and your neighbor as yourself. Seek gifts of the Holy Spirit. Share the gospel message by word and deed and by teaching the Word..

Lament over the things you need to repent. Cry, weep, grieve, and pray in the Spirit with groanings of the Holy Spirit.

Laugh after all at the end of the day the Lord is laughing at the wicked. See Psalm 2:4 Be thankful and grateful for everything. Enjoy your blessings. Always remember your name's written in heaven in the Lamb's book of Life!

I have seen the tagline **live, love, laugh** everywhere on cups, t-shirts, calendars, as headlines on blogs, podcasts, books, everywhere. Somehow, I've always thought that there was something missing. Where is the word **LAMENT**? That's what's missing. To live, love and laugh are all wonderful gifts from Father God Most High from whom all blessings flow through Christ Jesus. True repentance which is lamenting is needed when called for. We are all sinners in need of grace called to live a life of holiness and servitude for God. It's a personal choice to love God with our whole heart, soul, mind and strength and neighbor as ourself. Drawing close to God, we can fulfill our life's calling, choosing to work hard to make a living in a way that glorifies God. He wants us to enjoy our life with times of refreshing. It's about being balanced. *James 4:7-10*

[James 4:7-10 KJV] 7 **Submit yourselves therefore to God. Resist the devil,** and he will flee from you. 8 Draw nigh to God, and he will draw nigh to you. Cleanse [your] hands, [ye] sinners; and purify [your] hearts, [ye] double minded. 9 **Be afflicted, and mourn, and weep: let your laughter be turned to mourning, and [your] joy to heaviness**. 10 Humble yourselves in the sight of the Lord, and he shall lift you up.

For everything there's a time and a season.

But there's a time and place for everything. If you've been carrying around guilt and shame, repent, lament and let it go. Submit yourself to God, resist the devil and he will flee. It says when we draw close to God, He will draw close to us. *Eccl 3:1, James 4:7-10* I simply believe we must be reminded to not take some things lightly. The fear of God is a major key to drawing close to Him. *2Tim 4:3* 2 Cor 7:1 Eccl 9:7

[Psalm 33:18 NLT] 18 But the **LORD watches over those who fear him**, those who **rely on his unfailing love.**

[1Chron 29:11 NIV] 11 Yours, LORD, is the greatness and the power and the glory and the majesty and the splendor, **for everything in heaven and earth is yours.** Yours, LORD, is the kingdom; you are exalted as head over all.

[Prov 4:23 NIV] 23 Above all else, **guard your heart, for everything you do flows from it.** [Eccl 3:1 NIV] 1 **There is a time for everything, and a season for every activity under the heavens:**

[Luke 14:17 NIV] 17 At the time of the banquet he sent his servant to tell those who had been invited, *'Come, for everything is now ready.'*

Thou Hast Turned My Mourning into Gladness

I worshiped and danced with our beloved one night as I began recording myself singing **"Amazing Grace"**. My creative juices were flowing which led me to write a chorus forming a bridge to Amazing Grace. The added chorus is really a song within itself that I titled **"The Secret Place"**.

I'm always feeling grateful and thankful for God's grace and mercy provided by the blood that covers our sins. Jesus, himself being grace sits on the throne next to the Father. I worshiped Him at the throne of grace inside of the secret place. Halleluyah!!! None of us are perfect, yet, we can freely approach him boldly with humility. Isn't that all God asks of us, to graciously serve him with all of our heart, soul, mind and strength. Thank you Jesus for all the times you've invited me to dance with you in spite of my filthy rags. I'm grateful that you clothe me with your righteousness with gladness. *Psalm 30:11-12 compare Hebrews 4:16*

[Psalm 30:11-12 KJV] 11 Thou hast turned for me my mourning into dancing: thou hast put off my sackcloth, and girded me with gladness; 12 To the end that [my] glory may sing praise to thee, and not be silent. O LORD my God, I will give thanks unto thee for ever.

[Heb 4:16 KJV] 16 Let us therefore come boldly unto the throne of grace, that we may obtain mercy, and find grace to help in time of need.

AMAZING GRACE by John Newton

THE SECRET PLACE by Faye Cross

Verse 1 Amazing Grace how sweet the sound, that saved a wretch like me/ I once was lost but now I'm found, was blind but now I see

Chorus/Bridge: The Secret Place

Amazing Grace, the Secret place/ Where I can see YOUR lovely face/and in YOUR eyes peace draws me near/ to rest in YOU, there's no more fear/ and I worship YOU at the throne of grace, thank YOU Lord for Amazing Grace **(repeat)**

Verse 2 Twas grace that taught my heart to fear/ and grace my fears relieved/ How precious did that grace appear/ the hour I first believed

Repeat Chorus/Bridge: The Secret Place

Here's a link for the video on my YT channel:

https://youtu.be/Fff5F_5cdfc

Heart to Heart

May my meditations be sweet before you Jesus...

In this moment I leave behind any feelings of shame or condemnation as I come into this place, the chamber of intimacy with YOU my Beloved Husband. I can always expect to get here by FAITH knowing YOU await me here inside of my heart. As I draw close to you, I seek your presence rejoicing only in the truth as it is only found in YOU, the living Word of TRUTH. We must bear all things, every test that comes our way. We must hope for all things, in all the promises you have spoken to us, especially our blessed hope for the gathering of Israel. In our waiting for your coming, we must endure all things, all the way till the end.

I love your commandments. I'm captive to you Jesus, for I love your righteousness. I will dance with you forever as I'm moved by your goodness, faithfulness, loving kindness, the beauty of your holiness, mercy and grace. You are my Yeshua, my Salvation, my Beloved Husband. I love you Abba Father.

Thank you my beloved Jesus, for our heart to heart moments!!!

Joining You in Heavenly Matrimony

Thank you for calling me to be a part of the remnant. I'm happy to share the excitement and anticipation of New Jerusalem coming with the saints at YOUR return. All the faithful ones who long to be joined in heavenly matrimony to Jesus Our Yahshua, are already married to YOU inside of our heart. And those who have not made that heart commitment yet, by your grace will get there in due time. Thank you for the free gift of salvation, writing our names in the Lamb's book of life. Thank you forever more for the opened door to you and the Father's heart. Knowing the door is always open to us is such a blessing, but even more we are blessed beyond all measure knowing YOU won't hesitate to knock on the door of our heart when You want to initiate spending time with us. *Romans 5:1-2 Revelation 3:7-8*

Enjoy your Dance with the King of Kings!!!

I hope you've been inspired by my cherished journal of heart filled treasured moments and my testimony. Remember God promises to share with us some of His secrets, the deep profound things if we long to know them. Revelations in His Word align our heart with His through the indwelling Holy Spirit. Along the way I've shared with you a few object lessons.

They are foundational in truth in the simplest form. All for the purpose of helping someone, I revealed some private matters of my life as well as those fairly hidden inside the church. If I can help at least one person, it's all been worthwhile. It always helps to know you're not alone in your struggles. Sexual sin is one of the greatest challenges in this world. It can grip anyone and that includes not only singles, but married, divorced, young, old, doesn't matter your ethnicity or your economical status. Many suffer in silence, in their guilt and shame being addicted to pornography. I know what it's like to be in this kind of bondage but God…yes, but God can set you free as He did me. I can tell you there's freedom from all bondages of sin whatever shape or form it takes on. If you know that you're in bondage to something, know that our Savior loves you and wants you to lay all of your burdens on Him. His yoke is much lighter to carry. Yes, give it all to Him, get set free to enjoy your dance with Him. God is perfect but we can be perfect in Him if we abide in Him. If you know someone that's going through similar challenges, please recommend this book to them. Everyone, again I say, enjoy your dance with Abba Father Yah through Jesus Our Yahshua. Know that it will last forever into all eternity which is everything. And the best part is sharing in His glory as we get to taste and see that HE IS GOOD, always getting better with time, like fine wine in the perfection of time. Hallelu**YAH**!!!

Always and forever, to YAH be all the GLORY!!!

REFERENCES:

[1] https://www.gotquestions.org/life-Hezekiah.html

[2] https://www.gotquestions.org/King-Zedekiah.htm

[3] Wikipedia.org/Gautama Buddha

[4] C. Wesley E-Sword.com

[5] https://www.gotquestions.org/who-Baal.html

[6] https://www.merriam-webster.com

[7] https://www.parentcompany.com

[8] Vines Concise Dictionary of the Bible W.E. VINE Charis Bible College

[9] @Prophet Lovy "How to read the Word (bible) effectively"

https://www.youtube.com/watch?v=TFwHcRNxy_I

Book Cover Design by Faye A. Cross

Music available at faithgracecross.com
Facebook / faithgracecross

Ministry websites
www.morningmannawithlove.com
www.hopedevotion.org
www.mydancewiththeking.com

Published by Faye A. Cross
for Sarah Flows Publishing/ sarahflowspublishing@gmail.com